SENSE AND NONSENSE

Jerome K. Jerome

ALAN SUTTON

First published 1923

First published in this edition in the United Kingdom in 1991 by
Alan Sutton Publishing Limited · Phoenix Mill · Far Thrupp · Stroud
Gloucestershire

First published in this edition in the United States of America in 1991 by
Alan Sutton Publishing Inc. · Wolfeboro Falls · NH 03896–0848

British Library Cataloguing in Publication Data

Jerome, Jerome K. (Jerome Klapka) *1859–1927*
Sense and nonsense.
1. English prose. English prose
I. Title   II. Jerome, *Jerome K. 1859–1927. Miscellany of
sense and nonsense.*
828.807

ISBN 0-86299-922-7

Library of Congress Cataloging in Publication Data applied for

Cover photograph: On Leave *by Wilhelm Carl August Zimmer (courtesy
Memsing Gallery; photograph Fine Art Photographic Library Ltd.)*

Typeset in 10/11 Imprint.
Typesetting and origination by
Alan Sutton Publishing Limited.
Printed in Great Britain by
The Guernsey Press Company Limited,
Guernsey, Channel Islands.

CONTENTS

Dedication

TO THE GENTLE
GUIDE
WHO LETS ME EVER GO MY OWN WAY,
YET BRINGS ME RIGHT—

TO THE LAUGHTER-LOVING
PHILOSOPHER
WHO, IF HE HAS NOT RECONCILED ME TO BEARING THE
TOOTHACHE PATIENTLY, AT LEAST HAS TAUGHT ME THE
COMFORT THAT THIS EVEN WILL ALSO PASS—

TO THE GOOD
FRIEND
WHO SMILES WHEN I TELL HIM OF MY TROUBLES, AND WHO
WHEN I ASK FOR HELP, ANSWERS ONLY 'WAIT!'—

TO THE GRAVE-FACED
JESTER
TO WHOM ALL LIFE IS BUT A VOLUME OF OLD HUMOUR—

TO GOOD MASTER
TIME
THIS LITTLE WORK OF A POOR
PUPIL
IS DEDICATED

(*Three Men on the Bummel.*)

THE MAN WHO WAS A HOSPITAL

It was my liver that was out of order. I knew it was my liver that was out of order, because I had just been reading a patent liver-pill circular, in which were detailed the various symptoms by which a man could tell when his liver was out of order. I had them all.

It is a most extraordinary thing, but I never read a patent medicine advertisement without being impelled to the conclusion that I am suffering from the particular disease therein dealt with in its most virulent form. The diagnosis seems in every case to correspond exactly with all the sensations that I have ever felt.

I remember going to the British Museum one day to read up the treatment for some slight ailment of which I had a touch – hay fever, I fancy it was. I got down the book, and read all I came to read; and then, in an unthinking moment, I idly turned the leaves, and began to indolently study diseases, generally. I forget which was the first distemper I plunged into – some fearful, devastating scourge, I know – and, before I had glanced half down the list of 'premonitory symptoms,' it was borne in upon me that I had fairly got it.

I sat for a while, frozen with horror; and then, in the listlessness of despair, I again turned over the pages. I came to typhoid fever – read the symptoms – discovered that I had typhoid fever, must have had it for months without knowing it – wondered what else I had got; turned up St Vitus's Dance – found, as I expected, that I had that too, – began to get interested in my case, and determined to sift it to the bottom, and so started alphabetically – read up ague, and learnt that I was sickening for it, and that the acute stage would commence in about another fortnight. Bright's disease, I was relieved to find, I had only in a modified form, and, so far as that was concerned, I might live for years. Cholera I had, with severe complications; and diphtheria I seemed to have been born with. I plodded conscientiously through the twenty-six letters, and the only malady I could conclude I had not got was housemaid's knee.

I felt rather hurt about this at first; it seemed somehow to be a sort of slight. Why hadn't I got housemaid's knee? Why this invidious reservation? After a while, however, less grasping feelings prevailed. I reflected that I had every other known malady in the pharmacology, and I grew less selfish, and determined to do without housemaid's knee. Gout, in its most malignant stage, it would appear, had seized me without my being aware of it; and zymosis I had evidently been suffering with from boyhood. There were no more diseases after zymosis, so I concluded there was nothing else the matter with me.

I sat and pondered. I thought what an interesting case I must be from a medical point of view, what an acquisition I should be to a class! Students would have no need to 'walk the hospitals', if they had me. I was a hospital in myself. All they need do would be to walk round me, and, after that, take their diploma.

Then I wondered how long I had to live. I tried to examine myself. I felt my pulse. I could not at first find any pulse at all. Then, all of a sudden, it seemed to start off. I pulled out my watch and timed it. I made it a hundred and forty-seven to the minute. I tried to feel my heart. I could not feel my heart. It had stopped beating. I have since been induced to come to the opinion that it must have been there all the time, and must have been beating, but I cannot account for it. I patted myself all over my front, from what I call my waist up to my head, and I went a bit round each side, and a little way up the back. But I could not feel or hear anything. I tried to look at my tongue. I stuck it out as far as ever it would go, and I shut one eye, and tried to examine it with the other. I could only see the tip, and the only thing that I could gain from that was to feel more certain than before that I had scarlet fever.

I had walked into that reading-room a happy, healthy man. I crawled out a decrepit wreck.

I went to my medical man. He is an old chum of mine, and feels my pulse, and looks at my tongue, and talks about the weather, all for nothing, when I fancy I'm ill; so I thought I would do him a good turn by going to him now. 'What a doctor wants,' I said, 'is practice. He shall have me. He will get more practice out of me than out of seventeen hundred of your ordinary, commonplace patients, with only one or two diseases each.' So I went straight up and saw him, and he said:

'Well, what's the matter with you?'

I said:

'I will not take up your time, dear boy, with telling you what is the matter with me. Life is brief, and you might pass away before I had finished. But I will tell you what is *not* the matter with me. Why I have not got house-maid's knee, I cannot tell you; but the fact remains that I have not got it. Every-thing else, however, I *have* got.'

And I told him how I came to discover it all.

Then he opened me and looked down me,

It was my liver that was out of order.

and clutched hold of my wrist, and then he hit me over the chest when I wasn't expecting it – a cowardly thing to do, I call it – and immediately afterwards butted me with the side of his head. After that, he sat down and wrote out a prescription, and folded it up and gave it to me, and I put it in my pocket and went out.

I did not open it. I took it to the nearest chemist's and handed it in. The man read it, and then handed it back.

He said he didn't keep it.

I said:

'You are a chemist?'

He said:

'I am a chemist. If I was a co-operative stores and family hotel combined, I might be able to oblige you. Being only a chemist hampers me.'

I read the prescription. It ran:

> '1 lb. beefsteak, with
> 1 pt. bitter beer
> every 6 hours.
> 1 ten-mile walk every morning.
> 1 bed at 11 sharp every night.

And don't stuff your head with things you don't understand.'

I followed the directions, with the happy result – speaking for myself – that my life was preserved, and is still going on.

(*Three Men in a Boat.*)

UNDER CANVAS

Camping out in rainy weather is not pleasant.

It is evening. You are wet through, and there is a good two inches of water in the boat, and all the things are damp. You find a place on the banks that is not quite so puddly as other places you have seen, and you land and lug out the tent, and two of you proceed to fix it.

It is soaked and heavy, and it flops about, and tumbles down on you, and clings round your head and makes you mad. The rain is pouring steadily down all the time. It is difficult enough to fix a tent in dry weather: in wet, the task becomes herculean. Instead of helping you, it seems to you that the other man is simply playing the fool. Just as you get your side beautifully fixed, he gives it a hoist from his end, and spoils it all.

'Here! what are you up to?' you call out.

'What are *you* up to?' he retorts; 'leggo, can't you?'

'Don't pull it; you've got it all wrong, you stupid ass!' you shout.

'No, I haven't,' he yells back; 'let go your side!'

'I tell you you've got it all wrong!' you roar, wishing that you could get at him; and you give your ropes a lug that pulls all his pegs out.

'Ah, the bally idiot!' you hear him mutter to himself; and then comes a savage haul, and away goes your side. You lay down the mallet and start to go round and tell him what you think about the whole business, and, at the same time, he starts round in the same direction to come and explain his views to you. And you follow each other round and round, swearing at one another, until the tent tumbles down in a heap, and leaves you looking at each other across its ruins, when you both indignantly exclaim, in the same breath:

'There you are! what did I tell you?'

Meanwhile, the third man, who has been bailing out the boat, and who has spilled the water down his sleeve, and has been cursing away to himself steadily for the last ten minutes, wants to know what the thundering blazes you're playing at, and why the blarmed tent isn't up yet.

At last, somehow or other, it does get up, and you land the things. It is hopeless attempting to make a wood fire, so you light the methylated spirit stove and crowd round that.

Rainwater is the chief article of diet at supper. The bread is two-thirds rainwater, the beefsteak-pie is exceedingly rich in it, and the jam, and the butter, and the salt, and the coffee have all combined with it to make soup.

Your first impression is that the end of the world has come.

After supper, you find your tobacco is damp, and you cannot smoke. Luckily you have a bottle of the stuff that cheers and inebriates, if taken in proper quantity, and this restores to you sufficient interest in life to induce you to go to bed.

There you dream that an elephant has suddenly sat down on your chest, and that the volcano has exploded and thrown you down to the bottom of the sea – the elephant still sleeping peacefully on your bosom. You wake up and grasp the idea that something terrible really has happened. Your first impression is that the end of the world has come; and then you think that this cannot be, and that it is thieves and murderers, or else fire, and this opinion you express in the usual method. No help comes, however, and all you know is that thousands of people are kicking you, and you are being smothered.

Somebody else seems in trouble, too. You can hear his faint cries coming from underneath your bed. Determining, at all events, to sell your life dearly, you struggle frantically, hitting out right and left with arms and legs, and yelling lustily the while, and at last something gives way, and you find your head in the fresh air. Two feet off, you dimly observe a half-dressed ruffian, waiting to kill you, and you are preparing for a life-and-death struggle with him, when it begins to dawn upon you that it's Jim.

'Oh, it's you, is it?' he says, recognizing you at the same moment.

'Yes,' you answer, rubbing your eyes; 'what's happened?'

'Bally tent's blown down, I think,' he says. 'Where's Bill?'

Then you both raise up your voices and shout for 'Bill!' and the ground beneath you heaves and rocks, and the muffled voice that you heard before replies from out the ruin:

'Get off my head, can't you?'

And Bill struggles out, a muddy, trampled wreck, and in an unnecessarily aggressive mood – he being under the evident belief that the whole thing has been done on purpose.

(Three Men in a Boat.)

UNCLE PODGER HANGS A PICTURE

You never saw such a commotion up and down a house, in all your life, as when my Uncle Podger undertook to do a job. A picture would have come home from the frame-maker's, and be standing in the dining-room, waiting to be put up; and Aunt Podger would ask what was to be done with it, and Uncle Podger would say:

'Oh, you leave that to *me*. Don't you, any of you, worry yourselves about that. *I'll* do all that.'

And then he would take off his coat, and begin. He would send the girl out for sixpen'orth of nails, and then one of the boys after her to tell her what size to get; and, from that, he would gradually work down, and start the whole house.

'Now you go and get me my hammer, Will,' he would shout; 'and you bring me the rule, Tom; and I shall want the step-ladder, and I had better have a kitchen-chair, too; and, Jim! you run round to Mr Goggles, and tell him, "Pa's kind regards, and hopes his leg's better; and will he lend him his spirit-level?" And don't you go, Maria, because I shall want somebody to hold me the light; and when the girl comes back, she must go out again for a bit of picture-cord; and Tom! – where's Tom? – Tom, you come here; I shall want you to hand me up the picture.'

And then he would lift up the picture, and drop it, and it would come out of the frame, and he would try to save the glass, and cut himself; and then he would spring round the room, looking for his handkerchief. He could not find his handkerchief, because it was in the pocket of the coat he had taken off, and he did not know where he had put the coat, and all the house had to leave off looking for his tools, and start looking for his coat; while he would dance round and hinder them.

'Doesn't anybody in the whole house know where my coat is? I never came across such a set in all my life – upon my word I didn't. Six of you! – and you can't find a coat that I put down not five minutes ago! Well, of all the —'

Then he'd get up, and find that he had been sitting on it, and would call out:

'Oh, you can give it up! I've found it myself now. Might just as well ask the cat to find anything as expect you people to find it.'

And, when half an hour had been spent in tying up his finger, and a new glass had been got, and the tools, and the ladder, and the chair, and the candle had been brought, he would have another go, the whole family, including the girl and the charwoman, standing round in a semi-circle, ready to help. Two people would have to hold the chair, and a third would help him up on it, and hold him there, and a fourth would hand him a nail, and a fifth would pass him up the hammer, and he would take hold of the nail, and drop it.

'There!' he would say, in an injured tone, 'now the nail's gone.'

And we would all have to go down on our knees and grovel for it, while he would stand on the chair, and grunt, and want to know if he was to be kept there all the evening.

The nail would be found at last, but by that time he would have lost the hammer.

'Where's the hammer? What did I do with the hammer? Great heavens! Seven of you, gaping round there, and you don't know what I did with the hammer!'

We would find the hammer for him, and then he would have lost sight of the mark he had made on the wall, where the nail was to go in, and each of us had to get up on the chair, beside him, and see if we could find it; and we would each discover it in a different place, and he would call us all fools, one after another, and tell us to get down. And he would take the rule, and re-measure and find that he wanted half thirty-one and three-eighths inches from the corner, and would try to do it in his head, and go mad.

And we would all try to do it in our heads, and all arrive at different results, and sneer at one another. And in the general row, the original number would be forgotten, and Uncle Podger would have to measure it again.

He would use a bit of string this time, and at the critical moment, when the old fool was leaning over the chair at an angle of forty-five, and trying to reach a point three inches beyond what was possible for him to reach, the string would slip, and down he would slide on to the piano, a really fine musical effect being produced by the suddenness with which his head and body struck all the notes at the same time.

And Aunt Maria would say that she would not allow the children to stand round and hear such language.

At last, Uncle Podger would get the spot fixed again, and put the point of the nail on it with his left hand, and take the hammer in his right hand. And, with the first blow, he would smash his thumb, and drop the hammer, with a yell, on somebody's toes.

Aunt Maria would mildly observe that, next time Uncle Podger was going to hammer a nail into the wall, she hoped he'd let her know in time, so that she could make arrangements to go and spend a week with her mother while it was being done.

'Oh! you women, you make such a fuss over everything,' Uncle Podger would reply, picking himself up. 'Why, I *like* doing a little job of this sort.'

And then he would have another try, and, at the second blow, the nail would go clean through the plaster, and half the hammer after it, and Uncle Podger be precipitated against the wall with force nearly sufficient to flatten his nose.

'There you are,' he would say, stepping heavily off the chair on to the charwoman's corns.

Then we had to find the rule and the string again, and a new hole was made; and, about midnight, the picture would be up – very crooked and insecure, the wall for yards round looking as if it had been smoothed down with a rake, and everybody dead beat and wretched – except Uncle Podger.

'There you are,' he would say, stepping heavily off the chair on to the charwoman's corns, and surveying the mess he had made with evident pride. 'Why, some people would have had a man in to do a little thing like that!'

(Three Men in a Boat.)

THE RULE OF THE WORLD

It seems to be the rule of this world. Each person has what he doesn't want, and other people have what he does want.

Married men have wives, and don't seem to want them; and young single fellows cry out that they can't get them. Poor people who can hardly keep themselves have eight hearty children. Rich old couples, with no one to leave their money to, die childless.

Then there are girls with lovers. The girls that have lovers never want them. They say they would rather be without them, that they bother them, and why don't they go and make love to Miss Smith and Miss Brown, who are plain and elderly, and haven't got any lovers? They themselves don't want lovers. They never mean to marry.

It does not do to dwell on these things; it makes one so sad.

There was a boy at our school, we used to call him Sandford and Merton. His real name was Stivvings. He was the most extraordinary lad I ever came across. I believe he really liked study. He used to get into awful rows for sitting up in bed and reading Greek; and as for French irregular verbs, there was simply no keeping him away from them. He was full of weird and unnatural notions about being a credit to his parents and an honour to the school; and he yearned to win prizes, and grow up and be a clever man, and had all those sorts of weak-minded ideas. I never knew such a strange creature, yet harmless, mind you, as the babe unborn.

Well, that boy used to get ill about twice a week, so that he couldn't go to school. There never was such a boy to get ill as that Sandford and Merton. If there was any known disease going within ten miles of him, he had it, and had it badly. He would take bronchitis in the dog-days, and have hay-fever at Christmas. After a six weeks' period of drought, he would be stricken down with rheumatic fever; and he would go out in a November fog and come home with a sunstroke.

They put him under laughing-gas one year, poor lad, and drew all his teeth, and gave him a false set, because he suffered so terribly with toothache; and then it turned to neuralgia and ear-ache. He was never without a cold, except once for nine weeks while he had scarlet fever; and he always had chilblains. During the great cholera scare of 1871, our neighbourhood was singularly free from it. There was only one reputed case in the whole parish: that case was young Stivvings.

He had to stop in bed when he was ill, and eat chicken and custards and hot-house grapes; and he would lie there and sob, because they wouldn't let him do Latin exercises, and took his German grammar away from him.

And we other boys, who would have sacrificed ten terms of our school-life for the sake of being ill for a day, and had no desire whatever to give our parents any excuse for being stuck-up about us, couldn't catch so much as a stiff neck. We fooled about in draughts, and it did us good, and freshened us up; and we took things to make us sick, and they made us fat, and gave us an appetite. Nothing we could think of seemed to make us ill until the holidays began. Then, on the breaking-up day, we caught colds, and whooping cough, and all kinds of disorders, which lasted until the term recommenced; when, in spite of everything we could manoeuvre to the contrary, we would get suddenly well again, and be better than ever.

Such is life!

(Three Men in a Boat.)

HARRIS AND THE MAZE

Harris asked me if I'd ever been in the maze at Hampton Court. He said he went in once to show somebody else the way. He had studied it up in a map, and it was so simple that it seemed foolish – hardly worth the twopence charged for admission. Harris said he thought that map must have been got up as a practical joke, because it wasn't a bit like the real thing, and only misleading. It was a country cousin that Harris took in. He said:

'We'll just go in here, so that you can say you've been, but it's very simple. It's absurd to call it a maze. You keep on taking the first turning to the right. We'll just walk round for ten minutes, and then go and get some lunch.'

They met some people soon after they had got inside, who said they had been there for three-quarters of an hour, and had had about enough of it. Harris told them they could follow him, if they liked; he was just going in, and then should turn round and come out again. They said it was very kind of him, and fell behind, and followed.

They picked up various other people who wanted to get it over, as they went along, until they had absorbed all the persons in the maze. People who had given up all hopes of ever getting either in or out, or of ever seeing their home and friends again, plucked up courage at the sight of Harris and his party, and joined the procession, blessing him. Harris said he should judge there must have been twenty people, following him, in all; and one woman with a baby, who had been there all the morning, insisted on taking his arm, for fear of losing him.

Harris kept on turning to the right, but it seemed a long way, and his cousin said he supposed it was a very big maze.

'Oh, one of the largest in Europe,' said Harris.

'Yes, it must be,' replied the cousin, 'because we've walked a good two miles already.'

Harris began to think it rather strange himself, but he held on until, at last, they passed the half of a penny bun on the ground that Harris's cousin swore he had noticed there seven minutes ago. Harris said: 'Oh, impossible!' but the woman with the baby said, 'Not at all,' as she herself had taken it from the child, and thrown it down there, just before she met Harris. She also added that she wished she never had met Harris, and expressed an opinion that he was an impostor. That made Harris mad, and he produced his map, and explained his theory.

'The map may be all right enough,' said one of the party, 'if you know whereabouts in it we are now.'

Harris didn't know, and suggested that the best thing to do would be to go back to the entrance, and begin again. For the beginning again part of it there was not much enthusiasm; but with regard to the advisability of going back to the entrance there was complete unanimity, and so they turned, and trailed after Harris again, in the opposite direction. About ten minutes more passed, and then they found themselves in the centre.

Harris thought at first of pretending that that was what he had been aiming at; but the crowd looked dangerous, and he decided to treat it as an accident.

Anyhow, they had got something to start from then. They did know where they were, and the map was once more consulted, and the thing seemed simpler than ever, and off they started for the third time.

And three minutes later they were back in the centre again.

After that, they simply couldn't get anywhere else. Whatever way they turned brought them back to the middle. It became so regular at length, that some of the people stopped there, and waited for the others to take a walk round, and come back to them. Harris drew out his map again, after a while, but the sight of it only infuriated the mob, and they told him to go and curl his hair with it. Harris said that he couldn't help feeling that, to a certain extent, he had become unpopular.

They all got crazy at last, and sang out for the keeper, and the man came and climbed up the ladder outside, and shouted out directions to them. But all their heads were, by this time, in such a confused whirl that they were incapable of grasping

They did not know where they were, and the map was once more consulted.

anything, and so the man told them to stop where they were, and he would come to them. They huddled together, and waited; and he climbed down, and came in.

He was a young keeper, as luck would have it, and new to the business; and when he got in, he couldn't find them, and he wandered about, trying to get to them, and then *he* got lost. They caught sight of him, every now and then, rushing about the other side of the hedge, and he would see them, and rush to get to them, and they would wait there for about five minutes, and then he would reappear again in exactly the same spot, and ask them where they had been.

They had to wait till one of the old keepers came back from his dinner before they got out.

Harris said he thought it was a very fine maze, so far as he was a judge; and we agreed that we would try to get George to go into it, on our way back.

(Three Men in a Boat.)

It was round about the grounds of this old priory that Henry VIII. is said to have waited for and met Anne Boleyn.

HENRY VIII. GOES A-WOOING

There are the ruins of an old priory in the grounds of Ankerwyke House, which is close to Picnic Point, and it was round about the grounds of this old priory that Henry VIII. is said to have waited for and met Anne Boleyn. He also used to meet her at Hever Castle in Kent, and also somewhere near St Albans. It must have been difficult for the people of England in those days to have found a spot where these thoughtless young folk were *not* spooning.

Have you ever been in a house where there are a couple courting? It is most trying. You think you will go and sit in the drawing-room, and you march off there. As you open the door, you hear a noise as if somebody had suddenly recollected something, and, when you get in, Emily is over by the window, full of interest in the opposite side of the road, and your friend, John Edward, is at the other end of the room with his whole soul held in thrall by photographs of other people's relatives.

'Oh!' you say, pausing at the door, 'I didn't know anybody was here.'

'Oh! didn't you?' says Emily, coldly, in a tone which implies that she does not believe you.

You hang about for a bit, then you say:

'It's very dark. Why don't you light the gas?'

John Edward says, 'Oh!' he hadn't noticed it; and Emily says that papa does not like the gas lit in the afternoon.

You tell them one or two items of news, and give them your views and opinions on the Irish question; but this does not appear to interest them. All they remark on any subject is,

'Oh!' 'Is it?' 'Did he?' 'Yes,' and 'You don't say so!' And, after ten minutes of such style of conversation, you edge up to the door, and slip out, and are surprised to find that the door immediately closes behind you, and shuts itself, without your having touched it.

Half an hour later, you think you will try a pipe in the conservatory. The only chair in the place is occupied by Emily; and John Edward, if the language of clothes can be relied upon, has evidently been sitting on the floor. They do not speak, but they give you a look that says all that can be said in a civilized community; and you back out promptly and shut the door behind you.

You are afraid to poke your nose into any room in the house now; so, after walking up and down the stairs for a while, you go and sit in your own bedroom. This becomes uninteresting, however, after a time, and so you put on your hat and stroll out into the garden. You walk down the path, and as you pass the summer-house you glance in, and there are those two young idiots, huddled up into one corner of it; and they see you, and are evidently under the idea that, for some wicked purpose of your own, you are following them about.

'Why don't they make a special room for this sort of thing, and make people keep to it?' you mutter; and you rush back to the hall and get your umbrella and go out.

It must have been very much like this when that foolish boy Henry VIII. was courting his little Anne. People in Buckinghamshire would have come upon them unexpectedly when they were mooning round Windsor and Wraysbury, and have exclaimed, 'Oh! you here!' and Henry would have blushed and said, 'Yes; he'd just come over to see a man;' and Anne would have said, 'Oh, I'm so glad to see you! Isn't it funny? I've just met Mr Henry VIII. in the lane, and he's going the same way I am.'

Then those people would have gone away and said to themselves: 'Oh! we'd better get out of here while this billing and cooing is on. We'll go down to Kent.'

And they would go to Kent, and the first thing they would see in Kent when they got there would be Henry and Anne fooling round Hever Castle.

'Oh, drat this!' they would have said. 'Here, let's go away. I can't stand any more of it. Let's go to St Albans – nice quiet place, St Albans.'

And when they reached St Albans, there would be that wretched couple, kissing under the Abbey walls. Then these folks would go and be pirates until the marriage was over.

(Three Men in a Boat.)

THE THING THAT SPOILT THE PICTURE

It was a glorious day, and the lock was crowded; and, as is a common practice up the river, a speculative photographer was taking a picture of us all as we lay upon the rising waters.

I did not catch what was going on at first, and was, therefore, extremely surprised at noticing George hurriedly smooth out his trousers, ruffle up his hair, and stick his cap on in a rakish manner at the back of his head, and then, assuming an expression of mingled affability and sadness, sit down in a graceful attitude, and try to hide his feet.

My first idea was that he had suddenly caught sight of some girl he knew, and I looked about to see who it was. Everybody in the lock seemed to have been suddenly struck wooden. They were all standing or sitting about in the most quaint and curious attitudes I have ever seen off a Japanese fan. All the girls were smiling. Oh, they did look so sweet! And all the fellows were frowning, and looking stern and noble.

And then, at last, the truth flashed across me, and I wondered if I should be in time. Ours was the first boat, and it would be unkind of me to spoil the man's picture, I thought.

So I faced round quickly, and took up a position in the prow, where I leant with careless grace upon the hitcher, in an attitude suggestive of agility and strength. I arranged my hair with a curl over the forehead, and threw an air of tender wistfulness into my expression, mingled with a touch of cynicism, which I am told suits me.

As we stood, waiting for the eventful moment, I heard someone behind call out:

'Hi! look at your nose.'

I could not turn round to see what was the matter, and whose nose it was that was to be looked at. I stole a side-glance at George's nose! It was all right – at all events, there was nothing wrong with it that could be altered. I squinted down at my own, and that seemed all that could be expected also.

'Look at your nose, you stupid ass!' came the same voice again, louder.

And then another voice cried:

'Push your nose out, can't you, you – you two with the dog!'

Neither George nor I dared to turn round. The man's hand was on the cap, and the picture might be taken at any moment. Was it us they were calling to? What was the matter with our noses? Why were they to be pushed out!

But now the whole lock started yelling, and a stentorian voice from the back shouted:

'Look at your boat, sir; you in the red and black caps. It's your two corpses that will get taken in that photo, if you ain't quick.'

We looked then, and saw that the nose of our boat had got fixed under the woodwork of the lock, while the in-coming water was rising all around it, and tilting it up. In another moment we should be over. Quick as thought, we each seized an oar, and a vigorous blow against the side of the lock with the butt-ends released the boat, and sent us sprawling on our backs.

We did not come out well in that photograph, George and I. Of course, as was to be expected, our luck ordained it, that the man should set his wretched machine in motion at the precise moment that we were both lying on our backs with a wild expression of 'Where am I? and what is it?' on our faces, and our four feet waving madly in the air.

Our feet were undoubtedly the leading article in that photograph. Indeed, very little else was to be seen. They filled up the foreground entirely. Behind them, you caught glimpses of the other boats, and bits of the surrounding scenery; but everything and everybody else in the lock looked so utterly insignificant and paltry compared with our feet that all the other people felt quite ashamed of themselves, and refused to subscribe to the picture.

The owner of one steam launch, who had bespoke six copies, rescinded the order on seeing the negative. He said he would take them if anybody could show him his launch, but nobody could. It was somewhere behind George's right foot.

There was a good deal of unpleasantness over the business. The photographer thought we ought to take a dozen copies each, seeing that the photo was about nine-tenths us, but we declined. We said we had no objection to being photo'd full-length, but we preferred to be taken the right way up.

(Three Men in a Boat.)

GEORGE GETS UP TOO EARLY

George said that the same kind of thing, only worse, had happened to him some eighteen months ago, when he was lodging by himself in the house of a certain Mrs Gippings. He said his watch went wrong one evening, and stopped at a quarter-past eight. He did not know this at the time because, for some reason or other, he forgot to wind it up when he went to bed (an unusual occurence with him), and hung it up over his pillow without ever looking at the thing.

It was in the winter when this happened, very near the shortest day, and a week of fog into the bargain, so the fact that it was still very dark when George awoke in the morning was no guide to him as to the time. He reached up, and hauled down his watch. It was a quarter-past eight.

'Angels and ministers of grace defend us!' exclaimed George; 'and here have I got to be in the City by nine. Why didn't somebody call me? Oh, this is a shame!' And he flung the watch down, and sprang out of bed, and had a cold bath, and washed himself, and dressed himself, and shaved himself in cold water because there was not time to wait for the hot, and then rushed and had another look at the watch.

Whether the shaking it had received in being thrown down on the bed had started it, or how it was, George could not say, but certain it was that from a quarter-past eight it had begun to go, and now pointed to twenty minutes to nine.

George snatched it up, and rushed downstairs. In the sitting-room, all was dark and silent: there was no fire, no breakfast. George said it was a wicked shame of Mrs G., and he made up his mind to tell her what he thought of her when he came home in the evening. Then he dashed on his great-coat and hat, and seizing his umbrella, made for the front door. The door was not even unbolted. George anathematized Mrs G. for a lazy old woman, and thought it was very strange that people could not get up at a decent, respectable time, unlocked and unbolted the door, and ran out.

He ran hard for a quarter of a mile, and at the end of that distance it began to be borne in upon him as a strange and curious thing that there were so few people about, and that there were no shops open. It was certainly a very dark and foggy morning, but still it seemed an unusual course to stop all business on that account. *He* had to go to business: why should other people stop in bed merely because it was dark and foggy!

At length he reached Holborn. Not a shutter was down! not a bus was about! There were three men in sight, one of whom was a policeman; a market-cart full of cabbages, and a dilapidated looking cab. George pulled out his watch and looked at it: it was five minutes to nine! He stood still and counted his pulse. He stooped down and felt his legs. Then, with his watch still in his hand, he went up to the policeman, and asked him if he knew what the time was.

'What's the time?' said the man, eyeing George up and down with evident suspicion; 'why, if you listen you will hear it strike.'

George listened, and a neighbouring clock immediately obliged.

'But it's only gone three!' said George in an injured tone, when it had finished.

'Well, and how many did you want it to go?' replied the constable.

'Why, nine,' said George, showing his watch.

'Do you know where you live?' said the guardian of public order, severely.

George thought, and gave the address.

'Oh! that's where it is, is it?' replied the man; 'well, you take my advice and go there quietly, and take that watch of yours with you; and don't let's have any more of it.'

And George went home again, musing as he walked along, and let himself in.

At first, when he got in, he determined to undress and go to bed again; but when he thought of the re-dressing and re-washing, and the having of another bath, he determined he would not, but would sit up and go to sleep in the easy-chair.

But he could not get to sleep: he never felt more wakeful in his life; so he lit the lamp and got out the chess-board, and played himself a game of chess. But even that did not enliven him: it seemed slow somehow; so he gave up chess and tried to read. He did not seem able to take any sort of interest in reading either, so he put on his coat again and went out for a walk.

It was horribly lonesome and dismal, and all the policemen he met regarded him with undisguised suspicion, and turned their lanterns on him and followed him about, and this had such an effect upon him at last that he began to feel as if he really had done something, and he got to slinking down the by-streets and hiding in dark doorways when he heard the regulation flip-flop approaching.

Of course, this conduct made the force only more distrustful of him than ever, and they would come and rout him out and ask him what he was doing there;

Turned their lanterns on him and followed him about.

and when he answered, 'Nothing,' he had merely come out for a stroll (it was then four o'clock in the morning), they looked as though they did not believe him, and two plain-clothes constables came home with him to see if he really did live where he had said he did. They saw him go in with his key, and then they took up a position opposite and watched the house.

He thought he would light the fire when he got inside, and make himself some breakfast, just to pass away the time; but he did not seem able to handle anything from a scuttleful of coals to a teaspoon without dropping it or falling over it, and making such a noise that he was in mortal fear that it would wake Mrs G. up, and that she would think it was burglars and open the window and call 'Police!' and then those two detectives would rush in and handcuff him, and march him off to the police-court.

He was in a morbidly nervous state by this time, and he pictured the trial, and his trying to explain the circumstances to the jury, and nobody believing him, and his being sentenced to twenty years' penal servitude, and his mother dying of a broken heart. So he gave up trying to get breakfast, and wrapped himself up in his overcoat and sat in the easy-chair till Mrs G. came down at half-past seven.

He said he had never got up too early since that morning: it had been such a warning to him.

(Three Men in a Boat.)

THE POLITE ART OF BUYING BOOTS

'It is not a brilliant publication,' I remarked, handing the book back to George; 'it is not a book that personally I would recommend to any German about to visit England; I think it would get him disliked. But I have read books published in London for the use of English travellers abroad every whit as foolish. Some educated idiot, misunderstanding seven languages, would appear to go about writing these books for the misinformation and false guidance of modern Europe.'

'You cannot deny,' said George, 'that these books are in large request. They are bought by the thousand, I know. In every town in Europe there must be people going about talking this sort of thing.'

'Maybe,' I replied; 'but fortunately nobody understands them. I have noticed, myself, men standing on railway platforms and at street corners reading aloud from such books. Nobody knows what language they are speaking; nobody has the slightest knowledge of what they are saying. This is, perhaps, as well; were they understood they would probably be assaulted.'

George said: 'Maybe you are right; my idea is to see what would happen if they were understood. My proposal is to get to London early on Wednesday morning, and spend an hour or two going about and shopping with the aid of this book. There are one or two little things I want – a hat and a pair of bedroom slippers, among other articles. I want to try this sort of talk where I can properly judge its effect. I want to see how the foreigner feels when he is talked to in this way.'

It struck me as a sporting idea. In my enthusiasm I offered

to accompany him, and wait outside the shop. I said I thought that Harris would like to be in it, too – or rather outside.

George said that was not quite his scheme. His proposal was that Harris and I should accompany him into the shop. With Harris, who looks formidable, to support him, and myself at the door to call the police if necessary, he said he was willing to adventure the thing.

We walked round to Harris's, and put the proposal before him. He examined the book, especially the chapters dealing with the purchase of shoes and hats. He said:

'If George talks to any bootmaker or any hatter the things that are put down here, it is not support he will want; it is carrying to the hospital that he will need.'

That made George angry.

'You talk,' said George, 'as though I were a foolhardy boy without any sense. I shall select from the more polite and less irritating speeches; the grosser insults I shall avoid.'

This being clearly understood, Harris gave in his adhesion; and our start was fixed for early Wednesday morning.

We arrived at Waterloo a little after nine, and at once proceeded to put George's experiment into operation. Opening the book at the chapter entitled 'At the Cab Rank,' we walked up to a hansom, raised our hats, and wished the driver 'Good-morning'.

This man was not to be outdone in politeness by any foreigner, real or imitation. Calling to a friend named 'Charles' to 'hold the steed,' he sprang from his box, and returned to us a bow that would have done credit to Mr Turveydrop himself. Speaking apparently in the name of the nation, he welcomed us to England, adding a regret that Her Majesty was not at the moment in London.

We could not reply to him in kind. Nothing of this sort had been anticipated by the book. We called him 'coachman,' at which he again bowed to the pavement, and asked him if he would have the goodness to drive us to the Westminster Bridge road.

He welcomed us to England.

He laid his hand upon his heart, and said the pleasure would be his.

Taking the third sentence in the chapter, George asked him what his fare would be.

The question, as introducing a sordid element into the conversation, seemed to hurt his feelings. He said he never took money from distinguished strangers; he suggested a souvenir – a diamond scarf pin, a gold snuff-box, some little trifle of that sort by which he could remember us.

As a small crowd had collected, and as the joke was drifting rather too far in the cabman's direction, we climbed in without further parley, and were driven away amid cheers. We stopped the cab at a boot shop a little past Astley's Theatre that looked the sort of place we wanted. It was one of those overfed shops that the moment their shutters are taken down in the morning disgorge their goods all round them. Boxes of boots stood piled on the pavement or in the gutter opposite. Boots hung in festoons about its doors and windows. Its sun-blind was as some grimy vine, bearing bunches of black and brown boots. Inside, the shop was a bower of boots. The man, when we entered, was busy with a chisel and hammer opening a new crate full of boots.

George raised his hat, and said 'Good-morning.'

The man did not even turn round. He struck me from the first as a disagreeable man. He grunted something which might have been 'Good-morning,' or might not, and went on with his work.

George said: 'I have been recommended to your shop by my friend, Mr X.'

In response, the man should have said: 'Mr X. is a most worthy gentleman; it will give me the greatest pleasure to serve any friend of his.'

What he did say was: 'Don't know him: never heard of him.'

This was disconcerting. The book gave three or four methods of buying boots; George had carefully selected the one centred round 'Mr X.' as being of all the most courtly. You talked a good deal with the shopkeeper about this 'Mr X.', and then, when by this means friendship and understanding had been established, you slid naturally and gracefully into the immediate object of your coming, namely, your desire for boots, 'cheap and good'. This gross, material man cared, apparently, nothing for the niceties of retail dealing. It was necessary with such an one to come to business with brutal directness. George abandoned 'Mr X', and turning back to a previous page, took a sentence at random. It was not a happy selection; it was a speech that would have been superfluous made to any bootmaker. Under the present circumstances, threatened and stifled as we were on every side by boots, it possessed the dignity of positive imbecility. It ran:– 'One has told me that you have here boots for sale.'

For the first time the man put down his hammer and chisel,

and looked at us. He spoke slowly, in a thick and husky voice. He said:

'What d'ye think I keep boots for – to smell 'em?'

He was one of those men that begin quietly and grow more angry as they proceed, their wrongs apparently working within them like yeast.

'What d'ye think I am,' he continued, 'a boot collector? What d'ye think I'm running this shop for – my health? D'ye think I love the boots, and can't bear to part with a pair? D'ye think I hang 'em about here to look at 'em? Ain't there enough of 'em? Where d'ye think you are – in an international exhibition of boots? What d'ye think these boots are – a historical collection? Did you ever hear of a man keeping a boot shop and not selling boots? D'ye think I decorate the shop with 'em to make it look pretty? What d'ye take me for – a prize idiot?'

I have always maintained that these conversation books are never of any real use. What we wanted was some English equivalent for the well-known German idiom: 'Behalten Sie Ihr Haar auf.'

Nothing of the sort was to be found in the book from beginning to end. However, I will do George the credit to admit he chose the very best sentence that was to be found therein and applied it. He said:

'I will come again, when, perhaps, you will have some more boots to show me. Till then, adieu!'

(Three Men on the Bummel.)

VERBOTEN

Another passion you must restrain in Germany is that prompting you to throw things out of window. Cats are no excuse. During the first week of my residence in Germany I was awakened incessantly by cats. One night I got mad. I collected a small arsenal – two or three pieces of coal, a few hard pears, a couple of candle ends, an odd egg I found on the kitchen table, an empty soda-water bottle, and a few articles of that sort, – and, opening the window, bombarded the spot from where the noise appeared to come. I do not suppose I hit anything; I never knew a man who did hit a cat, even when he could see it, except, maybe, by accident when aiming at something else. I have known crack shots, winners of Queen's prizes – those sort of men, – shoot with shot-guns at cats fifty yards away, and never hit a hair. I have often thought that, instead of bull's-eyes, running deer, and that rubbish, the really superior marksman would be he who could boast that he had shot the cat.

But, anyhow, they moved off; maybe the egg annoyed them. I had noticed when I picked it up that it did not look a good egg; and I went back to bed again, thinking the incident closed. Ten minutes afterwards there came a violent ringing of the electric bell. I tried to ignore it, but it was too persistent, and, putting on my dressing gown, I went down to the gate. A policeman was standing there. He had all the things I had been throwing out of my window in a little heap in front of him, all except the egg. He had evidently been collecting them. He said:

'Are these things yours?'

I said: 'They were mine, but personally I have done with them. Anybody can have them – you can have them.'

He ignored my offer. He said:

'You threw these things out of window.'

'You are right,' I admitted; 'I did.'

'What cats?' he asked.

'Why did you throw them out of window?' he asked. A German policeman has his code of questions arranged for him; he never varies them, and he never omits one.

'I threw them out of the window at some cats,' I answered.

'What cats?' he asked.

It was the sort of question a German policeman would ask. I replied with as much sarcasm as I could put into my accent that I was ashamed to say I could not tell him what cats. I explained that, personally, they were strangers to me; but I offered, if the police would call all the cats in the district together, to come round and see if I could recognize them by their yaul.

The German policeman does not understand a joke, which is perhaps on the whole just as well, for I believe there is a heavy fine for joking with any German uniform; they call it 'treating an official with contumely.' He merely replied that it was not the duty of the police to help me recognize the cats; their duty was merely to fine me for throwing things out of window.

I asked what a man was supposed to do in Germany when woke up night after night by cats, and he explained that I could lodge an information against the owner of the cat, when the police would proceed to caution him, and, if necessary, order the cat to be destroyed. Who was going to destroy the cat, and what the cat would be doing during the process, he did not explain.

I asked him how he proposed I should discover the owner of the cat. He thought for a while, and then suggested that I might follow it home. I did not feel inclined to argue with him any more after that; I should only have said things that would have made the matter worse. As it was, that night's sport cost me twelve marks; and not a single one of the four German officials who interviewed me on the subject could see anything ridiculous in the proceedings from beginning to end.

(Three Men on the Bummel.)

MORNING AT 'BEGGARBUSH'

I knew that if he slept at 'Beggarbush' he would be up in time;
I have slept there myself, and I know what happens. About the
middle of the night, as you judge, though in reality it may be
somewhat later, you are startled out of your first sleep by what
sounds like a rush of cavalry along the passage, just outside
your door. Your half-wakened intelligence fluctuates between
burglars, the Day of Judgment, and a gas explosion. You sit up
in bed and listen intently. You are not kept waiting long; the
next moment a door is violently slammed, and somebody, or
something, is evidently coming downstairs on a tea-tray.

'I told you so,' says a voice outside, and immediately some
hard substance, a head one would say from the ring of it,
rebounds against the panel of your door.

By this time you are charging madly round the room for
your clothes. Nothing is where you put it overnight, the
articles most essential have disappeared entirely; and meanwhile the murder, or revolution, or whatever it is, continues
unchecked. You pause for a moment, with your head under the
wardrobe, where you think you can see your slippers, to listen
to a steady, monotonous thumping upon a distant door. The
victim, you presume, has taken refuge there; they mean to
have him out and finish him. Will you be in time? The
knocking ceases, and a voice, sweetly reassuring in its gentle
plaintiveness, asks meekly:

'Pa, may I get up?'

You do not hear the other voice, but the responses are:

'No, it was only the bath – no, she ain't really hurt, – only
wet, you know. Yes, ma, I'll tell 'em what you say. No, it was a

pure accident. Yes; good-night, papa.'

Then the same voice, exerting itself so as to be heard in a distant part of the house, remarks:

'You've got to come upstairs again. Pa says it isn't time yet to get up.'

You return to bed, and lie listening to somebody being dragged upstairs, evidently against their will. By a thoughtful arrangement the spare rooms at 'Beggarbush' are exactly underneath the nurseries. The same somebody, you conclude, still offering the most creditable opposition, is being put back into bed. You can follow the contest with much exactitude, because every time the body is flung down upon the spring mattress, the bedstead, just above your head, makes a sort of jump; while every time the body succeeds in struggling out again, you are aware by the thud upon the floor. After a time the struggle wanes, or maybe the bed collapses; and you drift back into sleep. But the next moment, or what seems to be the next moment, you again open your eyes under the consciousness of a presence. The door is being held ajar, and four solemn faces, piled one on top of the other, are peering at you, as though you were some natural curiosity kept in this particular room. Seeing you awake, the top face, walking calmly over the other three, comes in and sits on the bed in a friendly attitude.

'Oh!' it says, 'we didn't know you were awake. I've been awake some time.'

'So I gather,' you reply, shortly.

'Pa doesn't like us to get up too early,' it continues. 'He says everybody else in the house is liable to be disturbed if we get up. So, of course, we mustn't.'

The tone is one of gentle resignation. It is instinct with the spirit of virtuous pride, arising from the consciousness of self-sacrifice.

'Don't you call this being up?' you suggest.

'Oh, no; we're not really up, you know, because we're not

properly dressed.' The fact is self-evident. 'Pa's always very tired in the morning,' the voice continues; 'of course, that's because he works hard all day. Are you ever tired in the morning?'

At this point he turns and notices, for the first time, that the three other children have also entered, and are sitting in a semi-circle on the floor. From their attitude it is clear they have mistaken the whole thing for one of the slower forms of entertainment, some comic lecture or conjuring exhibition, and are waiting patiently for you to get out of bed and do something. It shocks him, the idea of their being in the guest's bedchamber. He peremptorily orders them out. They do not answer him, they do not argue; in dead silence, and with one accord they fall upon him. All you can see from the bed is a confused tangle of waving arms and legs, suggestive of an intoxicated octopus trying to find bottom. Not a word is spoken; that seems to be the etiquette of the thing. If you are sleeping in your pyjamas, you spring from the bed, and only add to the confusion; if you are wearing a less showy garment, you stop where you are and shout commands, which are utterly unheeded. The simplest plan is to leave it to the eldest boy. He does get them out after a while, and closes the door upon them. It re-opens immediately, and one, generally Muriel, is shot back into the room. She enters as from a catapult. She is handicapped by having long hair, which can be used as a convenient handle. Evidently aware of this natural disadvantage, she clutches it herself tightly in one hand, and punches with the other. He opens the door again, and cleverly uses her as a battering-ram against the wall of those without. You can hear the dull crash as her head enters among them, and scatters them. When the victory is complete, he comes back and resumes his seat on the bed. There is no bitterness about him; he has forgotten the whole incident.

'I like the morning,' he says, 'don't you?'

'Some mornings,' you agree, 'are all right; others are not so peaceful.'

He takes no notice of your exception; a far-away look steals over his somewhat ethereal face.

'I should like to die in the morning,' he says; 'everything is so beautiful then.'

'Well,' you answer, 'perhaps you will, if your father ever invites an irritable man to come and sleep here, and doesn't warn him beforehand.'

He descends from his comtemplative mood, and becomes himself again.

'It's jolly in the garden,' he suggests; 'you wouldn't like to get up and have a game of cricket, would you?'

It was not the idea with which you went to bed, but now, as things have turned out, it seems as good a plan as lying there hopelessly awake; and you agree.

You learn, later in the day, that the explanation of the proceeding is that you, unable to sleep, woke up early in the morning, and thought you would like a game of cricket. The children, taught to be ever courteous to guests, felt it their duty to humour you. Mrs Harris remarks at breakfast that at least you might have seen to it that the children were properly dressed before you took them out; while Harris points out to you, pathetically, how, by your one morning's example and encouragement, you have undone his labour of months.

(Three Men on the Bummel.)

THE WISDOM OF UNCLE PODGER

The wheel business settled, there arose the everlasting luggage question.

'The usual list, I suppose,' said George, preparing to write.

That was wisdom I had taught them. I had learned it myself years ago from my Uncle Podger.

'Always, before beginning to pack,' my Uncle would say, 'make a list.'

He was a methodical man.

'Take a piece of paper' – he always began at the beginning – 'put down on it everything you can possibly require; then go over it and see that it contains nothing you can possibly do without. Imagine yourself in bed; what have you got on? Very well, put it down – together with a change. You get up; what do you do? Wash yourself. What do you wash yourself with? Soap; put down soap. Go on till you have finished. Then take your clothes. Begin at your feet; what do you wear on your feet? Boots, shoes, socks; put them down. Work up till you get to your head. What else do you want besides clothes? A little brandy; put it down. A cork-screw; put it down. Put down everything, then you don't forget anything.'

That is the plan he always pursued himself. The list made, he would go over it carefully, as he always advised, to see that he had forgotten nothing. Then he would go over it again, and strike out everything it was possible to dispense with.

Then he would lose the list.

(Three Men on the Bummel.)

HARRIS TO THE RESCUE

The beautiful wood of the Eilenriede bounds Hanover on the south and west, and here occurred a sad drama in which Harris took a prominent part.

We were riding our machines through this wood on the Monday afternoon in the company of many other cyclists, for it is a favourite resort with the Hanoverians on a sunny afternoon, and its shady pathways are then filled with happy, thoughtless folk. Among them rode a young and beautiful girl on a machine that was new. She was evidently a novice on the bicycle. One felt instinctively that there would come a moment when she would require help, and Harris, with his accustomed chivalry, suggested that we should keep near her. Harris, as he occasionally explains to George and to myself, has daughters of his own, or, to speak more correctly, a daughter, who as the years progress will no doubt cease practising catherine wheels in the front garden, and will grow up into a beautiful and respectable young lady. This naturally

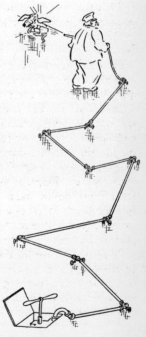

A man with a hose, watering the roads.

gives Harris an interest in all beautiful girls up to the age of thirty-five or thereabouts; they remind him, so he says, of home.

We had ridden for about two miles, when we noticed, a little ahead of us in a space where five ways met, a man with a hose, watering the roads. The pipe, supported at each joint by a pair of tiny wheels, writhed after him as he moved, suggesting a gigantic worm, from whose open neck, as the man, gripping it firmly with both hands, pointing it now this way, and now that, now elevating it, now depressing it, poured a strong stream of water at the rate of about a gallon a second.

'What a much better method than ours,' observed Harris enthusiastically. Harris is inclined to be chronically severe on all British institutions. 'How much simpler, quicker, and more economical! You see, one man by this method can in five minutes water a stretch of road that would take us with our clumsy lumbering cart half an hour to cover.'

George, who was riding behind me on the tandem, said, 'Yes, and it is also a method by which with a little carelessness a man could cover a good many people in a good deal less time than they could get out of the way.'

George, the opposite to Harris, is British to the core. I remember George quite patriotically indignant with Harris once for suggesting the introduction of the guillotine into England.

'It is so much neater,' said Harris.

'I don't care if it is,' said George; 'I'm an Englishman; hanging is good enough for me.'

'Our water-cart may have its disadvantages,' continued George, 'but it can only make you uncomfortable about the legs, and you can avoid it. This is the sort of machine with which a man can follow you round the corner and upstairs.'

'It fascinates me to watch them,' said Harris. 'They are so skilful. I have seen a man from the corner of a crowded square in Strassburg cover every inch of ground, and not so much as wet an apron string. It is marvellous how they judge their distance. They will send the water up to your toes, and then bring it over your head so that it falls around your heels. They can —'

'Ease up a minute,' said George.

I said: 'Why?'

He said: 'I am going to get off and watch the rest of this show from behind a tree. There may be great performers in this line, as Harris says; this particular artist appears to me to lack something. He has just soused a dog, and now he's busy watering a sign-post. I am going to wait till he has finished.'

'Nonsense,' said Harris; 'he won't wet you.'

'That is precisely what I am going to make sure of,' answered George, saying which he jumped off, and, taking up a position behind a remarkably fine elm, pulled out and commenced filling his pipe.

I did not care to take the tandem on by myself, so I stepped off and joined him, leaving the machine against a tree. Harris shouted something or other about our being a disgrace to the land that gave us birth, and rode on.

The next moment I heard a woman's cry of distress. Glancing round the stem of the tree, I perceived that it proceeded from the young and elegant lady before mentioned, whom, in our interest concerning the road-waterer, we had forgotten. She was riding her machine steadily and straightly through a drenching shower of water from the hose. She appeared to be too paralysed either to get off or turn her wheel aside. Every instant she was becoming wetter, while the man with the hose, who was either drunk or blind, continued to pour water upon her with utter indifference. A dozen voices yelled imprecations upon him, but he took no heed whatever.

Harris, his fatherly nature stirred to its depths, did at this point what, under the circumstances, was quite the right and proper thing to do. Had he acted throughout with the same coolness and judgment he then displayed, he would have emerged from that incident the hero of the hour, instead of, as happened, riding away followed by insult and threat. Without a moment's hesitation he spurted at the man, sprang to the ground, and, seizing the hose by the nozzle, attempted to wrest it away.

What he ought to have done, what any man retaining his common sense would have done the moment he got his hands upon the thing, was to turn off the tap. Then he might have played football with the man, or battledore and shuttlecock as he pleased; and the twenty or thirty people who had rushed forward to assist would have only applauded. His idea, however, as he explained to us afterwards, was to take away the hose from the man, and, for punishment, turn it upon the fool himself. The waterman's idea appeared to be the same, namely, to retain the hose as a weapon with which to soak Harris. Of course, the result was that, between them, they soused every dead and living thing for fifty yards, except themselves. One furious man, too drenched to care what more happened to him, leapt into the arena and also took a hand. The three among them proceeded to sweep the compass with that hose. They pointed it to heaven, and the water descended upon the people in the form of an equinoctial storm. They pointed it downwards, and sent the water in rushing streams that took people off their feet, or caught them about the waist line, and doubled them up.

Not one of them would loosen his grip upon the hose, not one of them thought to turn the water off. You might have concluded they were struggling with some primeval force of nature. In forty-five seconds, so George said, who was timing it, they had swept that circus bare of every living thing except one dog, who, dripping like a water nymph, rolled over by the force of water, now on this side, now on that, still gallantly staggered again and again to its feet to bark defiance at what it evidently regarded as the powers of hell let loose.

Men and women left their machines upon the ground, and

flew into the woods. From behind every tree of importance peeped out wet, angry heads.

At last, there arrived upon the scene one man of sense. Braving all things, he crept to the hydrant, where still stood the iron key, and screwed it down. And then from forty trees began to creep more or less soaked human beings, each one with something to say.

At first I fell to wondering whether a stretcher or a clothes basket would be the more useful for the conveyance of Harris's remains back to the hotel. I consider that George's promptness on that occasion saved Harris's life. Being dry, and therefore able to run quicker, he was there before the crowd. Harris was for explaining things, but George cut him short.

'You get on that,' said George, handing him his bicycle, 'and go. They don't know we belong to you, and you may trust us implicitly not to reveal the secret. We'll hang about behind, and get in their way. Ride zig-zag in case they shoot.'

(Three Men on the Bummel.)

UNCLE PODGER GOES TO TOWN

We caught the train by the skin of our teeth, as the saying is, and reflecting upon the events of the morning, as we sat gasping in the carriage, there passed vividly before my mind the panorama of my Uncle Podger, as on two hundred and fifty days in the year he would start from Ealing Common by the nine-thirteen train to Moorgate Street.

From my Uncle Podger's house to the railway station was eight minutes' walk. What my uncle always said was:

'Allow yourself a quarter of an hour, and take it easily.'

What he always did was to start five minutes before the time and run. I do not know why, but this was the custom of the suburb. Many stout City gentlemen lived at Ealing in those days – I believe some live there still – and caught early trains to Town. They all started late; they all carried a black bag and a newspaper in one hand, and an umbrella in the other; and for the last quarter of a mile to the station, wet or fine, they all ran.

Folks with nothing else to do, nursemaids chiefly and errand boys, with now and then a perambulating costermonger added, would gather on the common of a fine morning to watch them pass, and cheer the most deserving. It was not a showy spectacle. They did not run well, they did not even run fast; but they were earnest, and they did their best. The exhibition appealed less to one's sense of art than to one's natural admiration for conscientious effort.

Occasionally a little harmless betting would take place among the crowd.

'Two to one agin the old gent in the white weskit!'

'Ten to one on old Blowpipes, bar he don't roll over hisself 'fore 'e gets there!'

'Heven money on the Purple Hemperor!' – a nickname bestowed by a youth of entomological tastes upon a certain retired military neighbour of my uncle's, – a gentleman of imposing appearance when stationary, but apt to colour highly under exercise.

My uncle and the others would write to the *Ealing Press* complaining bitterly concerning the supineness of the local police; and the editor would add spirited leaders upon the Decay of Courtesy among the Lower Orders, especially throughout the Western Suburbs. But no good ever resulted.

It was not that my uncle did not rise early enough; it was that troubles came to him at the last moment.

The first thing he would do after breakfast would be to lose his newspaper. We always knew when Uncle Podger had lost anything, by the expression of astonished indignation with which, on such occasions, he would regard the world in general. It never occurred to my Uncle Podger to say to himself:

'I am a careless old man. I lose everything: I never know where I put anything. I am quite incapable of finding it again for myself. In this respect I must be a perfect nuisance to everybody about me. I must set to work and reform myself.'

On the contrary, by some peculiar course of reasoning,

he had convinced himself that whenever he lost a thing it was everybody else's fault in the house but his own.

'I had it in my hand here not a minute ago!' he would exclaim.

From his tone you would have thought he was living surrounded by conjurers, who spirited away things from him merely to irritate him.

'Could you have left it in the garden?' my aunt would suggest.

'What should I want to leave it in the garden for? I don't want a paper in the garden; I want the paper in the train with me.'

'You haven't put it in your pocket?'

'God bless the woman! Do you think I should be standing here at five minutes to nine looking for it if I had it in my pocket all the while? *Do* you think I'm a fool?'

Here somebody would exclaim, 'What's this?' and hand him from somewhere a paper neatly folded.

'I do wish people would leave my things alone,' he would growl, snatching at it savagely.

He would open his bag and put it in, and then glancing at it, he would pause, speechless with sense of injury.

'What's the matter?' aunt would ask.

'The day before yesterday's!' he would answer, too hurt even to shout, throwing the paper down upon the table.

If only sometimes it had been yesterday's it would have been a change. But it was always the day before yesterday's; except on Tuesday; then it would be Saturday's.

We would find it for him eventually; as often as not he was sitting on it. And then he would smile, not genially, but with the weariness that comes to a man who feels that fate has cast his lot among a band of hopeless idiots.

'All the time, right in front of your noses —!' He would not finish the sentence; he prided himself on his self-control.

(Three Men on the Bummel.)

A DISTURBER OF THE PEACE

An old corncrake lived near to us, and the way he used to disturb all the other birds, and keep them from going to sleep, was shameful. Amenda, who was town-bred, mistook him at first for one of those cheap alarm clocks, and wondered who was winding him up, and why they went on doing it all night; and, above all, why they didn't oil him.

He would begin his unhallowed performance about dusk, just as every respectable bird was preparing to settle down for the night. A family of thrushes had their nest a few yards from his stand, and they used to get perfectly furious with him.

'There's that fool at it again,' the female thrush would say; 'why can't he do it in the day-time if he must do it at all?' (She spoke, of course, in twitters, but I am confident the above is a correct translation.)

After a while, the young thrushes would wake up and begin chirping, and then the mother would get madder than ever.

'Can't you say something to

The way he used to disturb all the other birds and keep them from going to sleep was shameful.

him?' she would cry indignantly to her husband. 'How do you think the children can get to sleep, poor things, with that hideous row going on all night? Might just as well be living in a saw-mill.'

Thus adjured, the male thrush would put his head over the nest, and call out in a nervous, apologetic manner:

'I say, you know, you there, I wish you wouldn't mind being quiet a bit. My wife says she can't get the children to sleep. It's too bad, you know, 'pon my word it is.'

'Gor on,' the corncrake would answer surlily. 'You keep your wife herself quiet; that's enough for you to do.' And on he would go again worse than before.

Then a mother blackbird, from a little further off, would join in the fray.

'Ah, it's a good hiding he wants, not a talking to. And if I was a cock, I'd give it him.' (This remark would be made in a tone of withering contempt, and would appear to bear reference to some previous discussion.)

'You're quite right, ma'am,' Mrs Thrush would reply. 'That's what I tell my husband, but' (with rising inflection, so that every lady in the plantation might hear) '*he* wouldn't move himself, bless you – no, not if I and the children were to die before his eyes for want of sleep.'

'Ah, he ain't the only one, my dear,' the blackbird would pipe back, 'they're all alike'; then, in a voice more of sorrow than of anger: 'but there, it ain't their fault, I suppose, poor things. If you ain't got the spirit of a bird you can't help yourself.'

I would strain my ears at this point to hear if the male blackbird was moved at all by these taunts, but the only sound I could ever detect coming from his neighbourhood was that of palpably exaggerated snoring.

By this time the whole glade would be awake, expressing views concerning that corncrake that would have wounded a less callous nature.

'Blow me tight, Bill,' some vulgar little hedge-sparrow would chirp out, in the midst of the hubbub, 'if I don't believe the gent thinks 'e's a-singing.'

''Tain't 'is fault,' Bill would reply, with mock sympathy. 'Somebody's put a penny in the slot, and 'e can't stop 'isself.'

Irritated by the laugh that this would call forth from the younger birds, the corncrake would exert himself to be more objectionable than ever, and, as a means to this end, would commence giving his marvellous imitation of the sharpening of a rusty saw by a steel file.

But at this an old crow, not to be trifled with, would cry out angrily:

'Stop that, now. If I come down to you I'll peck your cranky head off, I will.'

And then would follow silence for a quarter of an hour, after which the whole thing would begin again.

(Novel Notes.)

THE PERFECT DANCER

This story comes from Furtwangen, a small town in the Black Forest. There lived there a wonderful old fellow named Nicholaus Geibel. His business was the making of mechanical toys, at which work he had acquired an almost European reputation. He made rabbits that would emerge from the heart of a cabbage, flap their ears, smooth their whiskers, and disappear again; cats that would wash their faces, and mew so naturally that dogs would mistake them for real cats, and fly at them; dolls, with phonographs concealed within them, that would raise their hats and say, 'Good morning; how do you do?' and some that would even sing a song.

But he was something more than a mere mechanic; he was an artist. His work was with him a hobby, almost a passion. His shop was filled with all manner of strange things that never would, or could, be sold – things that he made for the pure love of making them. He had contrived a mechanical donkey that would trot for two hours by means of stored electricity, and trot, too, much faster than the live article, and with less need for exertion on the part of the driver; a bird that would shoot up into the air, fly round and round in a circle, and drop to earth at the exact spot from where it started; a skeleton that, supported by an upright iron bar, would dance a hornpipe; a life-size lady doll that could play the fiddle; and a gentleman with a hollow inside who could smoke a pipe and drink more lager beer than any three average German students put together, which is saying much.

Indeed, it was the belief of the town that old Geibel could make a man capable of doing everything that a respectable man need want to do. One day he made a man who did too much, and it came about in this way.

Young Doctor Follen had a baby, and the baby had a birthday. Its first birthday put Doctor Follen's household into somewhat of a flurry, but on the occasion of its second birthday, Mrs Doctor Follen gave a ball in honour of the event. Old Geibel and his daughter Olga were among the guests.

During the afternoon of the next day, some three or four of Olga's bosom friends, who had also been present at the ball, dropped in to have a chat about it. They naturally fell to discussing the men, and to criticizing their dancing. Old Geibel was in the room, but he appeared to be absorbed in his newspaper, and the girls took no notice of him.

'There seem to be fewer men who can dance, at every ball you go to,' said one of the girls.

'Yes, and don't the ones who can give themselves airs,' said another; 'they quite make a favour of asking you.'

'And how stupidly they talk,' added a third. 'They always say exactly the same things: "How charming you are looking to-night." "Do you often go to Vienna?" "Oh, you should, it's delightful." "What a charming dress you have on." "What a warm day it has been." "Do you like Wagner?" I do wish they'd think of something new.'

'Oh, I never mind how they talk,' said a fourth. 'If a man dances well he may be a fool for all I care.'

'He generally is,' slipped in a thin girl, rather spitefully.

'I go to a ball to dance,' continued the previous speaker, not noticing the interruption. 'All I ask of a partner is that he shall hold me firmly, take me round steadily, and not get tired before I do.'

'A clockwork figure would be the thing for you,' said the girl who had interrupted.

'Bravo!' cried one of the others, clapping her hands, 'what a capital idea!'

'What's a capital idea?' they asked.

'Why, a clockwork dancer, or, better still, one that would go by electricity and never run down.'

The girls took up the idea with enthusiasm.

'Oh, what a lovely partner he would make,' said one; 'he would never kick you, or tread on your toes.'

'Or tear your dress,' said another.

'Or get out of step.'

'Or get giddy and lean on you.'

'And he would never want to mop his face with his handkerchief. I do hate to see a man do that after every dance.'

'And wouldn't want to spend the whole evening in the supper-room.'

'Why, with a phonograph inside him to grind out all the stock remarks, you would not be able to tell him from a real man,' said the girl who had first suggested the idea.

'Oh yes, you would,' said the thin girl, 'he would be so much nicer.'

Old Geibel had laid down his paper, and was listening with both his ears. On one of the girls glancing in his direction, however, he hurriedly hid himself again behind it.

After the girls were gone, he went into his workshop, where Olga heard him walking up and down, and every now and then chuckling to himself; and that night he talked to her a good deal about dancing and dancing men – asked what they usually said and did – what dances were the most popular – what steps were gone through, with many other questions bearing on the subject.

Then for a couple of weeks he kept much to his factory, and was very thoughtful and busy, though prone at unexpected moments to break into a quiet low laugh, as if enjoying a joke that nobody else knew of.

A month later another ball took place in Furtwangen. On this occasion it was given by old Wenzel, the wealthy timber merchant, to celebrate his niece's betrothal, and Geibel and his daughter were again among the invited.

When the hour arrived to set out, Olga sought her father. Not finding him in the house, she tapped at the door of his workshop. He appeared in his shirt-sleeves, looking hot, but radiant.

'Don't wait for me,' he said, 'you go on, I'll follow you. I've got something to finish.'

As she turned to obey he called after her, 'Tell them I'm going to bring a young man with me – such a nice young man, and an excellent dancer. All the girls will like him.' Then he laughed and closed the door.

Her father generally kept his doings secret from everybody, but she had a pretty shrewd suspicion of what he had been planning, and so, to a certain extent, was able to prepare the guests for what was coming. Anticipation ran high, and the arrival of the famous mechanist was eagerly awaited.

At length the sound of wheels was heard outside, followed by a great commotion in the passage, and old Wenzel himself, his jolly face red with excitement and suppressed laughter, burst into the room and announced in stentorian tones:

'Herr Geibel – and a friend.'

Herr Geibel and his 'friend' entered, greeted with shouts of laughter and applause, and advanced to the centre of the room.

'Allow me, ladies and gentlemen,' said Herr Geibel, 'to introduce to you my friend, Lieutenant Fritz. Fritz, my dear fellow, bow to the ladies and gentlemen.'

Geibel placed his hand encouragingly on Fritz's shoulder, and the lieutenant bowed low, accompanying the action with a harsh clicking noise in his throat, unpleasantly suggestive of a death rattle. But that was only a detail.

'He walks a little stiffly' (old Geibel took his arm and walked him forward a few steps. He certainly did walk stiffly), 'but then, walking is not his forte. He is essentially a dancing man. I have only been able to teach him the waltz as yet, but at that he is faultless. Come, which of you ladies may I introduce him to, as a partner? He keeps perfect time; he never gets tired; he won't kick you or tread on your dress; he will hold you as firmly as you like, and go as quickly or as slowly as you please; he never gets giddy; and he is full of conversation. Come, speak up for yourself, my boy.'

The old gentleman twisted one of the buttons of his coat, and immediately Fritz opened his mouth, and in thin tones that appeared to proceed from the back of his head, remarked suddenly, 'May I have the pleasure?' and then shut his mouth again with a snap.

That Lieutenant Fritz had made a strong impression on the company was undoubted, yet none of the girls seemed inclined to dance with him. They looked askance at his waxen face, with its staring eyes and fixed smile, and shuddered. At last old Geibel came to the girl who had conceived the idea.

'It is your own suggestion, carried out to the letter,' said Geibel, 'an electric dancer. You owe it to the gentleman to give him a trial.'

She was a bright saucy little girl, fond of a frolic. Her host added his entreaties, and she consented.

Herr Geibel fixed the figure to her. Its right arm was screwed round her waist, and held her firmly; its delicately jointed left hand was made to fasten itself upon her right. The old toymaker showed her how to regulate its speed, and how to stop it, and release herself.

'It will take you round in a complete circle,' he explained; 'be careful that no one knocks against you, and alters its course.'

The music struck up. Old Geibel put the current in motion, and Annette and her strange partner began to dance.

For a while everyone stood watching them. The figure performed its purpose admirably. Keeping perfect time and step, and holding its little partner tightly clasped in an unyielding embrace, it revolved steadily, pouring forth at the same time a constant flow of squeaky conversation, broken by brief intervals of grinding silence.

'How charming you are looking to-night,' it remarked in its thin, far-away voice. 'What a lovely day it has been. Do you like dancing? How well our steps agree. You will give me another, won't you? Oh, don't be so cruel. What a charming gown you have on. Isn't waltzing delightful? I could go on dancing for ever – with you. Have you had supper?'

As she grew more familiar with the uncanny creature the girl's nervousness wore off, and she entered into the fun of the thing.

'Oh, he's just lovely,' she cried, laughing, 'I could go on dancing with him all my life.'

Couple after couple now joined them, and soon all the dancers in the room were whirling round behind them. Nicholaus Geibel stood looking on, beaming with childish delight at his success.

Old Wenzel approached him, and whispered something in his ear. Geibel laughed and nodded, and the two worked their way quietly towards the door.

'This is the young people's house to-night,' said Wenzel, as soon as they were outside; 'you and I will have a quiet pipe and a glass of hock, over in the counting-house.'

Meanwhile the dancing grew more fast and furious. Little Annette loosened the screw regulating her partner's rate of progress, and the figure flew round with her swifter and swifter. Couple after couple dropped out exhausted, but they only went the faster, till at length they were the only pair left dancing.

Madder and madder became the waltz. The music lagged behind: the musicians, unable to keep pace, ceased, and sat staring. The younger guests applauded, but the older faces began to grow anxious.

'Hadn't you better stop, dear,' said one of the women, 'you'll make yourself so tired.'

But Annette did not answer.

'I believe she's fainted,' cried out a girl, who had caught

sight of her face as it was swept by.

One of the men sprang forward and clutched at the figure, but its impetus threw him down on to the floor, where its steel-cased feet laid bare his cheek. The thing evidently did not intend to part with its prize easily.

Had anyone retained a cool head, the figure, one cannot help thinking, might easily have been stopped. Two or three men, acting in concert, might have lifted it bodily off the floor, or have jammed it into a corner. But few heads are capable of remaining cool under excitement. Those who are not present think how stupid must have been those who were; those who are, reflect afterwards how simple it would have been to do this, that, or the other, if only they had thought of it at the time.

The women grew hysterical. The men shouted contradictory directions to one another. Two of them made a bungling rush at the figure, which had the result of forcing it out of its orbit in the centre of the room, and sending it crashing against the walls and furniture. A stream of blood showed itself down the girl's white frock, and followed her along the floor. The affair was becoming horrible. The women rushed screaming from the room. The men followed them.

One sensible suggestion was made: 'Find Geibel – fetch Geibel.'

No one had noticed him leave the room, no one knew where he was. A party went in search of him. The others, too unnerved to go back into the ball-room, crowded outside the door and listened. They could hear the steady whir of the wheels upon the polished floor, as the thing spun round and round; the dull thud as every now and again it dashed itself and its burden against some opposing object and ricocheted off in a new direction.

And everlastingly it talked in that thin ghostly voice, repeating over and over the same formula: 'How charming you are looking to-night. What a lovely day it has been. Oh, don't be so cruel. I could go on dancing for ever – with you. Have you had supper?'

Of course they sought for Geibel everywhere but where he was. They looked in every room in the house, then they rushed off in a body to his own place, and spent precious minutes in waking up his deaf old housekeeper. At last it occurred to one of the party that Wenzel was missing also, and then the idea of the counting-house across the yard presented itself to them, and there they found him.

He rose up, very pale, and followed them; and he and old Wenzel forced their way through the crowd of guests gathered outside, and entered the room, and locked the door behind them.

From within there came the muffled sound of low voices and quick steps, followed by a confused scuffling noise, then silence, then the low voices again.

After a time the door opened, and those near it pressed forward to enter, but old Wenzel's broad shoulders barred the way.

'I want you – and you, Bekler,' he said, addressing a couple of the elder men. His voice was calm, but his face was deadly white. 'The rest of you, please go – get the women away as quickly as you can.'

From that day old Nicholaus Geibel confined himself to the making of mechanical rabbits and cats that mewed and washed their faces.

(Novel Notes.)

WET TO STORMY

Houseboats then were not built to the scale of Mississippi steamers, but this boat was a small one, even for that primitive age. The man from whom we hired it described it as 'compact'. The man to whom, at the end of the first month, we tried to sub-let it, characterized it as 'poky'. In our letters we traversed this definition. In our hearts we agreed with it.

At first, however, its size – or, rather, its lack of size – was one of its chief charms in Ethelbertha's eyes. The fact that if you got out of bed carelessly you were certain to knock your head against the ceiling, and that it was utterly impossible for any man to put on his trousers except in the saloon, she regarded as a capital joke.

That she herself had to take a looking-glass and go upon the roof to do her back hair, she thought less amusing.

Amenda accepted her new surroundings with her usual philosophic indifference. On being informed that what she had mistaken for a linen-press was her bedroom, she remarked that there was one advantage about it, and that was that she could not tumble out of bed, seeing there was nowhere to tumble; and on being shown the kitchen, she observed that she should like it for two things – one was that she could sit in the middle and reach everything without getting up; the other, that nobody else could come into the apartment while she was there.

'You see, Amenda,' explained Ethelbertha apologetically, 'we shall really live outside.'

'Yes, mum,' answered Amenda, 'I should say that would be the best place to do it.'

If only we could have lived more outside, the life might have been pleasant enough, but the weather rendered it impossible, six days out of the seven, for us to do more than look out of the window and feel thankful that we had a roof over our heads.

I have known wet summers before and since. I have learnt by many bitter experiences the danger and foolishness of leaving the shelter of London any time between the first of May and the thirty-first of October. Indeed, the country is always associated in my mind with recollections of long, weary days passed in the pitiless rain, and sad evenings spent in other peoples' clothes. But never have I known, and never, I pray night and morning, may I know again, such a summer as the one we lived through (though none of us expected to) on that confounded houseboat.

In the morning we would be awakened by the rain's forcing its way through the window and wetting the bed, and would get up and mop out the saloon. After breakfast I would try to work, but the beating of the hail upon the roof just over my head would drive every idea out of my brain, and, after a wasted hour or two, I would fling down my pen and hunt up Ethelbertha, and we would put on our mackintoshes and take our umbrellas and go out for a row. At midday we would return and put on some dry clothes, and sit down to dinner.

In the afternoon the storm generally freshened up a bit, and we were kept pretty busy rushing about with towels and cloths, trying to prevent the water from coming into the rooms and swamping us. During tea-time the saloon was usually illuminated by forked lightning. The evenings were spent in bailing out the boat, after which we took it in turns to go into the kitchen and warm ourselves. At eight we supped, and from then until it was time to go to bed we sat wrapped up in rugs, listening to the roar of the thunder, and the howling of the wind, and the lashing of the waves, and wondering whether the boat would hold out through the night.

Friends would come down to spend the day with us –

We would put on our mackintoshes and take our umbrellas and go out for a row.

elderly, irritable people, fond of warmth and comfort; people who did not, as a rule, hanker after jaunts, even under the most favourable conditions; but who had been persuaded by our silly talk that a day on the river would be to them like a Saturday to Monday in Paradise.

They would arrive soaked, and we would shut them up in different bunks, and leave them to strip themselves and put on things of Ethelbertha's or of mine. But Ethel and I in those days were slim, so that stout, middle-aged people in our clothes neither looked well nor felt happy.

Upon their emerging we would take them into the saloon and try to entertain them by telling them what we had intended to do with them had the day been fine. But their answers were short, and occasionally snappy, and after a while the conversation would flag, and we would sit round reading last week's newspapers and coughing.

The moment their own clothes were dry (we lived in a perpetual atmostphere of steaming clothes) they would insist upon leaving us, which seemed to me discourteous after all that we had done for them, and would dress themselves once more and start off home, and get wet again before they got there.

We would generally receive a letter a few days afterwards, written by some relative, informing us that both patients were doing as well as could be expected, and promising to send us a card for the funeral in case of a relapse.

(Novel Notes.)

ON BABIES

Oh yes, I do – I know a lot about 'em. I was one myself once – though not long, not so long as my clothes. *They* were very long, I recollect, and always in my way when I wanted to kick. Why do babies have such yards of unnecessary clothing? It is not a riddle. I really want to know. I never could understand it. Is it that the parents are ashamed of the size of the child, and wish to make believe that it is longer than it actually is? I asked a nurse once why it was. She said——

'Lor', sir, they always have long clothes, bless their little hearts.'

And when I explained that her answer, although doing credit to her feelings, hardly disposed of my difficulty, she replied——

'Lor', sir, you wouldn't have 'em in *short* clothes, poor little dears?' And she said it in a tone that seemed to imply I had suggested some unmanly outrage.

Since then I have felt shy of making inquiries on the subject, and the reason – if reason there be – is still a mystery to me. But, indeed, putting them in any clothes at all seems absurd to my mind. Goodness knows, there is enough of dressing and undressing to be gone through in life, without beginning it before we need; and one would think that people who live in bed might, at all events, be spared the torture. Why wake the poor little wretches up in the morning to take one lot of clothes off, fix another lot on, and put them to bed again; and then, at night, haul them out once more, merely to change everything back? And when all is done, what difference is there, I should like to know, between a baby's nightshirt and the thing it wears in the day-time?

Very likely, however, I am only making myself ridiculous – I often do; so I am informed – and I will, therefore, say no more upon this matter of clothes, except only that it would be of great convenience if some fashion were adopted, enabling you to tell a boy from a girl.

At present it is most awkward. Neither hair, dress, nor conversation affords the slightest clue, and you are left to guess. By some mysterious law of Nature you invariably guess wrong, and are thereupon regarded by all the relatives and friends as a mixture of fool and knave, the enormity of alluding to a male babe as 'she' being only equalled by the atrocity of referring to a female infant as 'he'. Whichever sex the particular child in question happens *not* to belong to is considered as beneath contempt, and any mention of it is taken as a personal insult to the family.

Why do babies have such yards of unnecessary clothing?

And, as you value your fair name, do not attempt to get out of the difficulty by talking of 'it'. There are various methods by which you may achieve ignominy and shame. By murdering a large and respected family in cold blood, and afterwards depositing their bodies in the water companies' reservoir, you will gain much unpopularity in the neighbourhood of your crime, and even robbing a church will get you cordially disliked, especially by the vicar. But if you desire to drain to the dregs the fullest cup of scorn and hatred that a fellow human creature can pour out for you, let a young mother hear you call dear baby 'it'.

Your best plan is to address the article as 'little angel'. The noun 'angel' being of common gender, suits the case admirably, and the epithet is sure of being favourably received. 'Pet' or 'beauty' are useful for variety's sake, but 'angel' is the term that brings you the greatest credit for sense and good feeling. The word should be preceded by a short giggle, and accompanied by as much smile as possible. And, whatever you do, don't forget to say that the child has got its father's nose. This 'fetches' the parents (if I may be allowed a vulgarism) more than anything. They will pretend to laugh at the idea at first, and will say, 'Oh, nonsense!' You must then get excited, and insist that it is a fact. You need have no conscientious scruples on the subject, because the thing's nose really does resemble its father's – at all events quite as much as it does anything else in nature – being, as it is, a mere smudge.

Do not despise these hints, my friends. There may come a time when, with mamma on one side and grandmamma on the other, a group of admiring young ladies (not admiring you, though) behind, and a bald-headed dab of humanity in front, you will be extremely thankful for some idea of what to say. A man – an unmarried man, that is – is never seen to such disadvantage as when undergoing the ordeal of 'seeing baby'. A cold shudder runs down his back at the bare proposal, and the sickly smile with which he says how delighted he shall be, ought surely to move even a mother's heart, unless, as I am inclined to believe, the whole proceeding is a mere device, adopted by wives to discourage the visits of bachelor friends.

It is a cruel trick, though, whatever its excuse may be. The bell is rung, and somebody sent to tell nurse to bring baby down. This is the signal for all the females present to commence talking 'baby', during which time you are left to your own sad thoughts and to speculations upon the practicability of suddenly recollecting an important engagement, and the likelihood of your being believed if you do. Just when you have concocted an absurdly implausible tale about a man outside, the door opens, and a tall, severe-looking woman enters, carrying what at first sight appears to be a particularly skinny bolster, with the feathers all at one end. Instinct, however, tells you that this is the baby, and you rise with a miserable attempt at appearing eager. When the first gush of feminine enthusiasm with which the object in question is received has died out, and the number of ladies talking at once has been reduced to the ordinary four or five, the circle of fluttering petticoats divides, and room is made for you to step forward. This you do with much the same air that you would walk into the dock at Bow Street, and then, feeling unutterably miserable, you stand solemnly staring at the child. There is dead silence, and you know that everyone is waiting for you to speak. You try to think of something to say, but find, to your horror, that your reasoning faculties have left you. It is a moment of despair, and your evil genius, seizing the opportunity, suggests to you some of the most idiotic remarks that it is possible for a human being to perpetrate. Glancing round with an imbecile smile, you sniggeringly observe that, 'It hasn't got much hair, has it?' Nobody answers you for a minute, but at last the stately nurse says with much gravity – 'It is not customary for children five weeks old to have long hair.' Another silence follows this, and you feel you are being given a second chance, which you avail yourself of by inquiring if it can walk yet, or what they feed it on.

By this time, you have got to be regarded as not quite right in your head, and pity is the only thing felt for you. The nurse, however, is determined that, insane or not, there shall be no shirking, and that you shall go through your task to the end. In the tones of a high priestess, directing some religious mystery, she says, holding the bundle towards you, 'Take her in your arms, sir.' You are too crushed to offer any resistance, and so meekly accept the burden. 'Put your arm more down her middle, sir,' says the high priestess, and then all step back and watch you intently as though you were going to do a trick with it.

What to do you know no more than you did what to say. It is certain something must be done, however, and the only thing that occurs to you is to heave the unhappy infant up and down to the accompaniment of 'oopsee-daisy', or some remark of equal intelligence. 'I wouldn't jig her, sir, if I were you,' says the nurse; 'a very little upsets her.' You promptly decide *not* to jig her, and sincerely hope that you have not gone too far already.

At this point, the child itself, who has hitherto been regarding you with an expression of mingled horror and disgust, puts an end to the nonsense by beginning to yell at the top of its voice, at which the priestess rushes forward and snatches it from you with, 'There, there, there! What did ums do to ums?' 'How very extraordinary!' you say pleasantly. 'Whatever made it go off like that?' 'Oh, why you must have done something to her!' says the mother indignantly; 'the child wouldn't scream like that for nothing.' It is evident they think you have been running pins into it.

The brat is calmed at last, and would no doubt remain quiet enough, only some mischievous busybody points you out again with, 'Who's this, baby?' and the intelligent child, recognizing you, howls louder than ever.

Whereupon, some fat old lady remarks that, 'It's strange how children take a dislike to anyone.' 'Oh, *they* know,' replies another mysteriously. 'It's a wonderful thing,' adds a third; and then everybody looks sideways at you, convinced you are a scoundrel of the blackest dye; and they glory in the beautiful idea that your true character, unguessed by your fellowmen, has been discovered by the untaught instinct of a little child.

(Idle Thoughts of an Idle Fellow.)

CATS AND DOGS

They are much superior to human beings as companions. They do not quarrel or argue with you. They never talk about themselves, but listen to you while you talk about yourself, and keep up an appearance of being interested in the conversation. They never make stupid remarks. They never observe to Miss Brown across a dinner-table, that they always understood she was very sweet on Mr Jones (who has just married Miss Robinson). They never mistake your wife's cousin for her husband, and fancy that you are the father-in-law. And they never ask a young author with fourteen tragedies, sixteen comedies, seven farces, and a couple of burlesques in his desk why he doesn't write a play.

They never say unkind things. They never tell us of our faults, 'merely for our own good'. They do not, at inconvenient moments, mildly remind us of our past follies and mistakes. They do not say, 'Oh yes, a lot of use *you* are, if you are ever really wanted' – sarcastic like. They never inform us, like our *inamoratas* sometimes do, that we are not nearly so nice as we used to be. We are always the same to them.

They are always glad to see us. They are with us in all our humours. They are merry when we are glad, sober when we feel solemn, sad when we are sorrowful.

'Hulloa! happy, and want a lark! Right you are; I'm your man. Here I am, frisking round you, leaping, barking, pirouetting, ready for any amount of fun and mischief. Look at my eyes, if you doubt me. What shall it be? A romp in the drawing-room, and never mind the furniture, or a scamper in the fresh, cool air, a scud across the fields, and down the hill, and won't we let old Gaffer Goggles's geese know what time o' day it is, neither. Whoop! come along.'

Or you'd like to be quiet and think. Very well. Pussy can sit on the arm of the chair, and purr, and Montmorency will curl himself up on the rug, and blink at the fire, yet keeping one eye on you the while, in case you are seized with any desire in the direction of rats.

And when we bury our face in our hands and wish we had never been born, they don't sit up very straight, and observe that we have brought it all upon ourselves. They don't even hope it will be a warning to us. But they come up softly; and shove their heads against us. If it is a cat, she stands on your shoulder, rumples your hair, and says, 'Lor', I am sorry for you, old man,' as plain as words can speak; and if it is a dog, he looks up at you with his big, true eyes, and says with them, 'Well, you've always got me, you know. We'll go through the world together, and always stand by each other, won't we?'

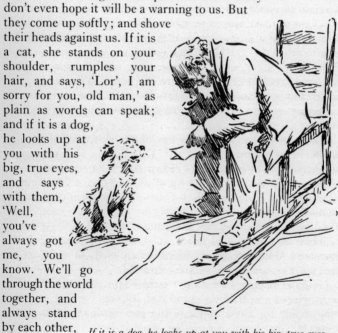

If it is a dog, he looks up at you with his big, true eyes, and says with them, 'Well, you've always got me, you know.'

He is very

imprudent, a dog is. He never makes it his business to inquire whether you are in the right or in the wrong, never bothers as to whether you are going up or down upon life's ladder, never asks whether you are rich or poor, silly or wise, sinner or saint. You are his pal. That is enough for him, and, come luck or misfortune, good repute or bad, honour or shame, he is going to stick to you, to comfort you, guard you, give his life for you, if need be – foolish, brainless, soulless dog!

Ah! old staunch friend, with your deep, clear eyes, and bright, quick glances, that take in all one has to say before one has time to speak it, do you know you are only an animal, and have no mind? Do you know that that dull-eyed, gin-sodden lout, leaning against the post out there, is immeasurably your intellectual superior? Do you know that every little-minded, selfish scoundrel, who lives by cheating and tricking, who never did a gentle deed, or said a kind word, who never had a thought that was not mean and low, or a desire that was not base, whose every action is a fraud, whose every utterance is a lie; do you know that these crawling skulks (and there are millions of them in the world), do you know they are all as much superior to you as the sun is superior to rushlight, you honourable, brave-hearted, unselfish brute? They are MEN, you know, and MEN are the greatest, and noblest, and wisest, and best Beings in the whole vast eternal Universe. Any man will tell you that.

Yes, poor doggie, you are very stupid, very stupid indeed, compared with us clever men, who understand all about politics and philosophy, and who know everything, in short, except what we are, and where we came from, and whither we are going, and what everything outside this tiny world and most things in it are.

(Idle Thoughts of an Idle Fellow.)

A CHARMING WOMAN

'Not *the* Mr——, *really?*'

In her deep brown eyes there lurked pleased surprise, struggling with wonder. She looked from myself to the friend who introduced us with a bewitching smile of incredulity, tempered by hope.

He assured her, adding laughingly, 'The only genuine and original,' and left us. 'I've always thought of you as a staid, middle-aged man,' she said, with a delicious little laugh, then added in low soft tones, 'I'm so very pleased to meet you, really.'

'I've always thought of you as a staid, middle-aged man.'

The words were conventional, but her voice crept round one like a warm caress.

'Come and talk to me,' she said, seating herself upon a small settee, and making room for me.

I sat down awkwardly beside her, my head buzzing just a little as with one glass too many of champagne. I was in my literary childhood. One small book and a few essays and criticisms, scattered through various obscure periodicals had been as yet my only contributions to current literature. The sudden discovery that I was *the* Mr Anybody, and that charming women thought of me, and were delighted to meet me, was a brain-disturbing thought.

'And it was really you who wrote that clever book?' she continued, 'and all those brilliant things in the magazines and journals. Oh, it must be delightful to be clever.'

She gave breath to a little sigh of vain regret that went to my heart. To console her I commenced a laboured compliment, but she stopped me with her fan. On after reflection I was glad she had – it would have been one of those things better expressed otherwise.

'I know what you are going to say,' she laughed, 'but don't. Besides, from you I should not know quite how to take it. You can be so satirical.'

I tried to look as though I could be, but in her case would not.

She let her ungloved hand rest for an instant upon mine. Had she left it there for two, I should have gone down on my knees before her, or have stood on my head at her feet – have made a fool of myself in some way or another before the whole room full. She timed it to a nicety.

'I don't want *you* to pay me compliments,' she said, 'I want us to be friends. Of course, in years, I'm old enough to be your mother.' (By the register I should say she might have been thirty-two, but looked twenty-six. I was twenty-three, and I fear foolish for my age.) 'But you know the world, and you're

so different to the other people one meets. Society is so hollow
and artificial; don't you find it so? You don't know how I long
sometimes to get away from it, to know someone to whom I
could show my real self, who would understand me. You'll
come and see me sometimes – I'm always at home on
Wednesdays – and let me talk to you, won't you, and you must
tell me all your clever thoughts.'

It occurred to me that, maybe, she would like to hear a few
of them there and then, but before I had got well started a
hollow Society man came up and suggested supper, and she
was compelled to leave me. As she disappeared, however, in
the throng, she looked back over her shoulder with a glance
half pathetic, half comic, that I understood. It said, 'Pity me,
I've got to be bored by this vapid, shallow creature,' and I did.

I sought her through all the rooms before I went. I wished to
assure her of my sympathy and support. I learned, however,
from the butler that she had left early, in company with the
hollow Society man.

A fortnight later I ran against a young literary friend in
Regent Street, and we lunched together at the Monico.

'I met such a charming woman last night,' he said, 'a Mrs
Clifton Courtenay, a delightful woman.'

'Oh, do *you* know her?' I exclaimed. 'Oh, we're very old
friends. She's always wanting me to go and see her. I really
must.'

'Oh, I didn't know *you* knew her,' he answered. Somehow,
the fact of my knowing her seemed to lessen her importance in
his eyes. But soon he recovered his enthusiasm for her.

'A wonderfully clever woman,' he continued. 'I'm afraid I
disappointed her a little though.' He said this, however, with a
laugh that contradicted his words. 'She would not believe I was
the Mr Smith. She imagined from my book that I was quite an
old man.'

I could see nothing in my friend's book myself to suggest
that the author was, of necessity, anything over eighteen. The

mistake appeared to me to display want of acumen, but it had evidently pleased him greatly.

'I felt sorry for her,' he went on, 'chained to that bloodless, artificial society in which she lives. "You can't tell," she said to me, "how I long to meet someone to whom I can show my real self – who would understand me." I'm going to see her on Wednesday.'

I went with him. My conversation with her was not as confidential as I had anticipated, owing to there being some eighty other people present in a room intended for the accommodation of eight; but after surging round for an hour in hot and aimless misery – as very young men at such gatherings do, knowing as a rule only the man who has brought them, and being unable to find him – I contrived to get a few words with her.

She greeted me with a smile, in the light of which I at once forgot my past discomfort, and let her fingers rest, with delicious pressure, for a moment upon mine.

'How good of you to keep your promise,' she said. 'These people have been tiring me so. Sit here, and tell me all you have been doing.'

She listened for about ten seconds, and then interrupted me with –

'And that clever friend of yours that you came with. I met him at dear Lady Lennon's last week. Has *he* written anything?'

I explained to her that he had.

'Tell me about it,' she said. 'I get so little time for reading, and then I only care to read the books that help me,' and she gave a grateful look more eloquent than words.

I described the work to her, and wishing to do my friend justice I even recited a few of the passages upon which, as I knew, he especially prided himself.

One sentence in particular seemed to lay hold of her. 'A good woman's arms round a man's neck is a lifebelt thrown out to him from heaven.'

'How beautiful!' she murmured. 'Say it again.'

I said it again, and she repeated it after me.

Then a noisy old lady swooped down upon her, and I drifted away into a corner, where I tried to look as if I were enjoying myself, and failed.

Later on, feeling it time to go, I sought my friend, and found him talking to her in a corner. I approached and waited. They were discussing the latest East End murder. A drunken woman had been killed by her husband, a hard-working artisan, who had been maddened by the ruin of his home.

'Ah,' she was saying, 'what power a woman has to drag a man down or lift him up. I never read a case in which a woman is concerned without thinking of those beautiful lines of yours: 'A good woman's arms round a man's neck is a lifebelt thrown out to him from heaven.'

(Sketches in Lavender.)

CHOOSING A PROFESSION

A coffee-shop becomes a bit of a desert towards three o'clock; and, after a while, young Tidelman, for that was his name, got to putting down his book and chatting to me. His father was dead; which, judging from what he told me about the old man, must have been a bit of luck for everybody; and his mother, it turned out, had come from my own village in Suffolk; and that constituted a sort of bond between us, seeing I had known all her people pretty intimately. He was earning good money at a dairy, where his work was scouring milk-cans; and his Christian name – which was the only thing Christian about him, and that, somehow or other, didn't seem to fit him – was Joseph.

One afternoon he came into the shop looking as if he had lost a shilling and found sixpence, as the saying is; and instead of drinking water as usual, sent the girl out for a pint of ale. The moment it came he drank off half of it at a gulp, and then sat staring out of the window.

'What's up?' I says. 'Got the shove?'

'Yes,' he answers; 'but, as it happens, it's a shove up. I've been taken off the yard and put on the walk, with a rise of two bob a week.' Then he took another pull at the beer and looked more savage than ever.

'Well,' I says, 'that ain't the sort of thing to be humpy about.'

'Yes, it is,' he snaps back; 'it means that if I don't take precious good care I'll drift into being a blooming milkman, spending my life yelling "Milk ahoi!" and spooning smutty-faced servant-gals across area railings.'

'Oh!' I says, 'and what may you prefer to spoon – duchesses?'

'Yes,' he answers sulky-like; 'duchesses are right enough – some of 'em.'

'So are servant-gals,' I says, 'some of 'em. Your hat's feeling a bit small for you this morning, ain't it?'

'Hat's all right,' says he; 'it's the world as I'm complaining of – beastly place; there's nothing to do in it.'

'Oh!' I says; 'some of us find there's a bit too much.' I'd been up since five that morning myself; and his own work, which was scouring milk-cans for twelve hours a day, didn't strike me as suggesting a life of leisured ease.

'I don't mean that,' he says. 'I mean things worth doing.'

'Well, what do you want to do,' I says, 'that this world ain't big enough for?'

'It ain't the size of it,' he says; 'it's the dulness of it. Things used to be different in the old days.'

'How do you know?' I says.

'You can read about it,' he answers.

'Oh,' I says, 'and what do they know about it – these gents that sit down and write about it for their living! You show me a book cracking up the old times, writ by a chap as lived in 'em, and I'll believe you. Till then I'll stick to my opinion that the old days were much the same as these days, and maybe a trifle worse.'

'From a Sunday School point of view, perhaps yes,' says he; 'but there's no gainsaying—'

'No what?' I says.

'No gainsaying,' repeats he; 'it's a common word in literatoor.'

'Maybe,' says I, 'but this happens to be "The Blue Posts Coffee House," established in the year 1863. We will use modern English here, if you don't mind.' One had to take him down like that at times. He was the sort of boy as would talk poetry to you if you weren't firm with him.

'Well, then, there's no denying the fact,' says he, 'if you prefer it that way, that in the old days there was more opportunity for adventure.'

'What about Australia?' says I.

'Australia!' retorts he; 'what would I do there? Be a shepherd, like you see in the picture, wear ribbons, and play the flute?'

'There's not much of that sort of shepherding over there,' says I, 'unless I've been deceived; but if Australia ain't sufficiently uncivilized for you, what about Africa?'

'What's the good of Africa?' replies he; 'you don't read advertisements in the *Clerkenwell News:* "Young men wanted as explorers." I'd drift into a barber's shop at Capetown more likely than anything else.'

'What about the gold diggings?' I suggests. I like to see a youngster with the spirit of adventure in him. It shows grit as a rule.

'Played out,' says he. 'You are employed by a company, wages ten dollars a week, and a pension for your old age. Everything's played out,' he continues. 'Men ain't wanted nowadays. There's only room for clerks, and intelligent artisans, and shopboys.'

'Go for a soldier,' says I, 'there's excitement for you.'

'That would have been all right,' says he, 'in the days when there was real fighting.'

'There's a good bit of it going about nowadays,' I says. 'We are generally at it, on and off, between shouting about the blessings of peace.'

'Not the sort of fighting I mean,' replies he; 'I want to do something myself, not be one of a row.'

'Well,' I says, 'I give you up. You've dropped into the wrong world it seems to me. We don't seem able to cater for you here.'

'I've come a bit too late,' he answers; 'that's the mistake I've made. Two hundred years ago there were lots of things a fellow might have done.'

'Yes, I know what's in your mind,' I says, 'pirates.'

'Yes, pirates would be all right,' says he; 'they got plenty of sea-air and exercise, and didn't need to join a blooming funeral club.'

82

'You've got ideas above your station,' I says. 'You work hard, and one day you'll have a milk-shop of your own, and be walking out with a pretty housemaid on your arm, feeling as if you were the Prince of Wales himself.'

'Stow it!' he says; 'it makes me shiver for fear it might come true. I'm not cut out for a respectable cove, and I won't be one neither, if I can help it!'

'What do you mean to be then?' I says; 'we've all got to be something, until we're stiff 'uns.'

'Well,' he says, quite cool-like, 'I think I shall be a burglar.'

I dropped into the seat opposite and stared at him. If any other lad had said it I should have known it was only foolishness, but he was just the sort to mean it.

'It's the only calling I can think of,' says he, 'that has got any element of excitement left in it.'

'You call seven years at Portland "excitement," do you?' says I, thinking of the argument most likely to tell upon him.

'Yes, I know what's in your mind,' I says, 'pirates.'

'What's the difference,' answers he, 'between Portland and the ordinary labouring man's life, except that at Portland you never need fear being out of work?' He was a rare one to argue. 'Besides,' says he, 'it's only the fools as gets copped. Look at that diamond robbery in Bond Street, two years ago. Fifty thousand pounds worth of jewels stolen, and never a clue to this day! Look at the Dublin Bank robbery,' says he, his eyes all alight, and his face flushed like a girl's. 'Three thousand pounds in golden sovereigns walked away with in broad daylight, and never so much as the flick of a coat-tail seen. Those are the sort of men I'm thinking of, not the bricklayer out of work, who smashes a window and gets ten years for breaking open a cheesemonger's till with nine and fourpence ha'penny in it.'

'Yes,' says I, 'and are you forgetting the chap who was nabbed at Birmingham only last week? He wasn't exactly an amatoor. How long do you think he'll get?'

'A man like that deserves what he gets,' answers he; 'couldn't hit a policeman at six yards.'

'You bloodthirsty young scoundrel,' I says; 'do you mean you wouldn't stick at murder?'

'It's all in the game,' says he, not in the least put out. 'I take my risks, he takes his. It's no more murder than soldiering is.'

'It's taking a human creature's life,' I says.

'Well,' he says, 'what of it? There's plenty more where he comes from.'

I tried reasoning with him from time to time, but he wasn't a sort of boy to be moved from a purpose. His mother was the only argument that had any weight with him. I believe so long as she lived he would have kept straight; that was the only soft spot in him. But unfortunately she died a couple of years later, and then I lost sight of Joe altogether. I made enquiries, but no one could tell me anything. He had just disappeared, that's all.

(Observations of Henry and Others.)

HOW TO GO TO BED IN GERMANY

We went to bed after our wash. To the *blasé* English bed-goer, accustomed all his life to the same old hackneyed style of bed night after night, there is something very pleasantly piquant about the experience of trying to sleep in a German bed. He does not know it is a bed at first. He thinks that someone has been going round the room, collecting all the sacks and cushions and anti-macassars and such articles that he has happened to find about, and has piled them up on a wooden tray ready for moving. He rings for the chambermaid, and explains to her that she has shown him into the wrong room. He wanted a bedroom.

She says: 'This *is* a bedroom.'

He says: 'Where's the bed?'

'There!' she says, pointing to the box on which the sacks and anti-macassars and cushions lie piled.

'That!' he cries. 'How am I going to sleep in that?'

The chambermaid does not know how he is going to sleep

there, never having seen a gentleman go to sleep anywhere, and not knowing how they set about it; but suggests that he might try lying down flat, and shutting his eyes.

'But it is not long enough,' he says.

The chambermaid thinks he will be able to manage, if he tucks his legs up.

He sees that he will not get anything better, and that he must put up with it.

'Oh, very well!' he says. 'Look sharp and get it made, then.'

She says: 'It is made.'

He turns and regards the girl sternly. Is she taking advantage of his being a lonely stranger, far from home and friends, to mock him? He goes over to what she calls the bed, and snatching off the top-most sack from the pile and holding it up, says:

'Perhaps you will tell me what this is, then?'

'That,' says the girl; 'that's the bed!'

He is somewhat nonplussed at the unexpected reply.

'Oh!' he says. 'Oh! the bed is it? I thought it was a pincushion! Well, if it is the bed, then what is it doing out here, on the top of everything else? You think that because I'm only a man, I don't understand a bed!'

'That's the proper place for it,' responds the chambermaid.

'What! on top?'

'Yes, sir.'

'Well, then, where are the clothes?'

'Underneath, sir.'

'Look here, my good girl,' he says; 'you don't understand me, or I don't understand you, one or the other. When I go to sleep, I lie on a bed and pull the clothes over me. I don't want to lie on the clothes, and cover myself with the bed. This isn't a comic ballet, you know!'

The girl assures him that there is no mistake about the matter at all. There is the bed, made according to German notions of how a bed should be made. He can make the best of it and try to go to sleep upon it, or he can be sulky and go to sleep on the floor.

He is very much surprised. It looks to him the sort of bed that a man would make for himself on coming home late from a party. But it is no use arguing the matter with the girl.

'All right,' he says; 'bring me a pillow, and I'll risk it!'

The chambermaid explains that there are two pillows on the bed already, indicating, as she does so, two flat cushions, each a yard square, placed one on top of the other at each end of the mixture.

'These!' exclaims the weary traveller, beginning to feel that he does not want to go to bed at all. 'These are not pillows! I want something to put my head on; not a thing that comes down to the middle of my back! Don't tell me that I've got to sleep on these things!'

But the girl does tell him so, and also implies that she has something else to do than to stand there all day talking bed-gossip with him.

'Well, just show me how to start,' he says, 'which way you get into it, and then I won't keep you any longer; I'll puzzle out the rest for myself.'

She explains the trick to him and leaves, and he undresses and crawls in.

The pillows give him a good deal of worry. He does not know whether he is meant to sit on them or merely to lean up against them. In experimenting upon this point, he bumps his head against the top board of the bedstead. At this, he says, 'Oh!' and shoots himself down to the bottom of the bed. Here all his ten toes simultaneously come into sharp contact with the board at the bottom.

Nothing irritates a man more than being rapped over the toes, especially if he feels that he has done nothing to deserve it. He says, 'Oh, damn!' this time, and spasmodically doubles up his legs, thus giving his knees a violent blow against the board at the side of the bed. (The German bedstead, be it remembered, is built in the form of a shallow, open box, and the victim is thus completely surrounded by solid pieces of wood with sharp edges. I do not know what species of wood it is that is employed. It is extremely hard, and gives forth a curious musical sound when struck sharply with a bone.)

After this he lies perfectly still for a while, wondering where he is going to be hit next. Finding that nothing happens, he begins to regain confidence, and ventures to gently feel around with his left leg and take stock of his position.

For clothes, he has only a very thin blanket and sheet, and beneath these he feels decidedly chilly. The bed is warm enough, so far as it goes, but there is not enough of it. He draws it up round his chin, and then his feet begin to freeze. He pushes it down over his feet, and then all the top part of him shivers.

He tries to roll up into a ball, so as to get the whole of himself underneath it, but does not succeed; there is always some of him left outside in the cold.

He reflects that a 'boneless wonder' or a 'man serpent' would be comfortable enough in this bed, and wishes that he had been brought up as a contortionist. If he could only tie his legs round his neck, and tuck his head in under his arm, all would yet be well.

Never having been taught to do any really useful tricks such as these, however, he has to be content to remain spread out, warming a bit of himself at a time.

It is, perhaps, foolish of him, amid so many real troubles, to allow a mere aesthetical consideration to worry him, but as he lies there on his back, looking down at himself, the sight that he presents to himself considerably annoys him. The puffed-up bed, resting on the middle of him, gives him the appearance of a man suffering from some monstrous swelling, or else of some exceptionally well-developed frog that has been turned up the wrong way and does not know how to get on to its legs again.

Another vexation that he has to contend with is, that every time he moves a limb or breathes extra hard, the bed (which is only of down) tumbles off on to the floor.

You cannot lean out of a German bed to pick up anything off the floor, owing to its box-like formation; so he has to scramble out after it, and of course every time he does this he barks both his shins twice against the sides of the bed.

When he has performed this feat for about the tenth time, he concludes that it was madness for him, a mere amateur at the business, to think that he could manage a complicated, tricky bed of this sort, that must take even an experienced man all he knows to sleep in it; and gets out and camps on the floor.

(Diary of a Pilgrimage.)

AT OBER-AMMERGAU

We ourselves saw the play yesterday and are now discussing it. I am explaining to B. the difficulty I experience in writing an account of it for my diary. I tell him that I really do not know what to say about it.

'Give them the history of the Passion Play,' he suggests, 'how it came to be played.'

'Oh, but so many people have done that already,' I say again.

'So much the better for you,' is his reply. 'Having previously heard precisely the same story from half a dozen other sources, the public will be tempted to believe you when you repeat the account. Tell them that during the Thirty Years' War a terrible plague (as if half a dozen different armies, marching up and down their country, fighting each other about the Lord only knows what, and living on them while doing it, was not plague enough) swept over Bavaria, devastating each town and hamlet. Of all the highland villages, Ober-Ammergau by means of a strictly enforced quarantine alone kept, for a while, the black foe at bay. No soul was allowed to leave the village; no living thing to enter it.

'But one dark night Caspar Schuchler, an inhabitant of Ober-Ammergau, who had been away working in the plague-stricken neighbouring village of Eschenlohe, creeping low on his belly, passed the drowsy sentinels, and gained his home, and saw what for many a day he had been hungering for – a sight of his wife and bairns. It was a selfish act to do, and he and his fellow-villagers paid dearly for it. Three days after he had entered his house he and all his family lay dead, and the plague was raging through the valley, and nothing seemed able to stay its course.

'When human means fail, we feel it is only fair to give Heaven a chance. The good people who dwelt by the side of the Ammer vowed that, if the plague left them, they would, every ten years, perform a Passion Play. The celestial powers seem to have at once closed with this offer. The plague disappeared as if by magic, and every recurring tenth year since, the Ober-Ammergauites have kept their promise and played their Passion Play. They act it to this day as a pious observance. Before each performance all the characters gather together on the stage around their pastor, and, kneeling, pray for a blessing upon the work then about to commence. The profits that are made, after paying the performers a wage that just compensates them for their loss of time – wood-carver Maier, who plays the Christ, only receives about fifty pounds for the whole of the thirty or so performances given during the season, to say nothing of the winter's rehearsals – is put aside, part for the temporal benefit of the community, and the rest for the benefit of the Church. From Burgomaster down to shepherd lad, from the Mary and the Jesus down to the meanest super, all work for the love of their religion, not for money. Each one feels that he is helping forward the cause of Christianity.'

'And I could also speak,' I add, 'of grand old Daisenberger, the gentle, simple old priest, "the father of the valley," who now lies in silence among his children that he loved so well. It was he, you know, that shaped the rude burlesque of a coarser age into the impressive reverential drama that we saw yesterday. That is a portrait of him over the bed. What a plain, homely, good face it is! How pleasant, how helpful it is to come across a good face now and then! I do not mean a sainted face, suggestive of stained glass and marble tombs, but a rugged human face that has had the grit, and rain, and sunshine of life rubbed into it, and that has gained its expression not by looking up with longing at the stars, but by looking down with eyes full of laughter and love at the human things around it.'

'Yes,' assented B. 'You can put in that if you like. There is no harm in it. And then you can go on to speak of the play itself, and give your impressions concerning it. Never mind their being silly. They will be all the better for that. Silly remarks are generally more interesting than sensible ones.'

'But what is the use of saying anything about it at all?' I urge. 'The merest schoolboy must know all about the Ober-Ammergau Passion Play by this time.'

'What has that to do with you?' answers B. 'You are not writing for cultured schoolboys. You are writing for mere simple men and women. They will be glad of a little information on the subject, and then when the schoolboy comes homes for his holiday they will be able, so far as this topic, at all events, is concerned, to converse with him on his own level and not appear stupid.

'Come,' he says, kindly, trying to lead me on, 'what did you think about it?'

'Well,' I reply, after musing for a while, 'I think that a play of eighteen acts and some forty scenes, which commences at eight o'clock in the morning, and continues, with an interval of an hour and a half for dinner, until six o'clock in the evening, is too long. I think the piece wants cutting. About a third of it is impressive and moving, and what the earnest student of the drama at home is for ever demanding that a play should be – namely, elevating; but I consider that the other two-thirds are tiresome.'

'Quite so,' answers B. 'But then we must remember that the performance is not intended as an entertainment, but as a religious service. To criticize any part of it as uninteresting, is like saying that half the Bible might very well have been omitted, and that the whole story could have been told in a third of the space.'

'And now, as to the right or wrong of the performance as a whole. Do you see any objection to the play from a religious point of view?'

'No,' I reply, 'I do not; nor do I understand how anybody else, and least of all a really believing Christian, can either. To argue as some do, that Christianity should be treated as a sacred mystery, is to argue against the whole scheme of Christianity. It was Christ himself that rent the veil of the Temple, and brought religion down into the streets and market-places of the world. Christ was a common man. He lived a common life, among common men and women. He died a common death. His own methods of teaching were what a Saturday reviewer, had he to deal with the case, would undoubtedly term vulgar. The roots of Christianity are planted deep down in the very soil of life, amid all that is common-place, and mean, and petty, and everyday. Its strength lies in its simplicity, its homely humanness. It has spread itself through the world by speaking to the hearts, rather than to the heads of men. If it is still to live and grow, it must be helped along by such methods as these peasant players of Ober-Ammergau employ, not by high-class essays and the learned discussions of cultured.

'The crowded audience that sat beside us in the theatre yesterday saw Christ of Nazareth nearer than any book, however inspired, could bring him to them; clearer than any words, however eloquent, could show him. They saw the sorrow of his patient face. They heard his deep tones calling to them. They saw him in the hour of his so-called triumph, wending his way through the narrow streets of Jerusalem, the multitude that thronged round him waving their branches of green palms and shouting loud hosannas.

'What a poor scene of triumph! – a poor-clad, pale-faced man, mounted upon the back of a shuffling unwilling little grey donkey, passing slowly through the byways of a city, busy upon other things. Beside him, a little band of worn, anxious men, clad in thread-bare garments – fishermen, petty clerks, and the like; and, following, a noisy rabble, shouting, as crowds in all lands and in all times shout, and as dogs bark, they know not why – because others are shouting, or barking. And that scene marks the highest triumph won while he lived on earth by the village carpenter of Galilee, about whom the world has been fighting and thinking and talking so hard for the last eighteen hundred years.

'They were present at the parting of Mary and Jesus by Bethany, and it will be many a day before the memory of that scene ceases to vibrate in their hearts. It is the scene that brings the humanness of the great tragedy most closely home to us. Jesus is going to face sorrow and death at Jerusalem. Mary's instinct tells her that this is so, and she pleads him to stay.

'Poor Mary! To others he is the Christ, the Saviour of mankind, setting forth upon his mighty mission to redeem the world. To loving Mary Mother, he is her son: the baby she has suckled at her breast, the little one she has crooned to sleep upon her lap, whose little cheek has lain against her heart, whose little feet have made sweet music through the poor home at Bethany: he is her boy, her child; she would wrap her mother's arms around him, and hold him safe against all the world, against even heaven itself.

'Never, in any human drama, have I witnessed a more moving scene than this. Never has the voice of any actress (and I have seen some of the greatest, if any great ones are living) stirred my heart as did the voice of Rosa Lang, the Burgo-master's daughter. It was not the voice of one woman, it was the voice of Motherdom, gathered together from all the world over.

'Oliver Wendell Holmes, in *The Autocrat of the Breakfast Table,* I think, confesses to having been bewitched at different times by two women's voices, and adds that both these voices belonged to German women. I am not surprised at either statement of the good doctor's. I am sure if a man did fall in love with a voice, he would find, on tracing it to its source, that it was the voice of some homely-looking German woman. I have never heard such exquisite soul-drawing music in my life, as I have more than once heard float from the lips of some sweet-faced German Fraulein when she opened her mouth to speak. The voice has been so pure, so clear, so deep, so full of soft caressing tenderness, so strong to comfort, so gentle to soothe, it has seemed like one of those harmonies musicians tell us that they dream of, but can never chain to earth.

'As I sat in the theatre, listening to the wondrous tones of this mountain peasant-woman, rising and falling like the murmur of a sea, filling the vast sky-covered building with their yearning notes, stirring like a great wind stirs Aeolian strings, the thousands of trembling hearts around her, it seemed to me that I was indeed listening to the voice of the "mother of the world," of mother Nature herself.

'They saw him, as they had often seen him in pictures, sitting for the last time with his disciples at supper. But yesterday they saw him, not a mute, moveless figure, posed in conventional, meaningless attitude, but a living, loving man, sitting in fellowship with the dear friends that against all the world had believed in him, and had followed his poor fortunes, talking with them for the last sweet time, comforting them.

'They heard him bless the bread and wine that they themselves to this day take in remembrance of him.

'They saw his agony in the Garden of Gethsemane, the human shrinking from the cup of pain. They saw the false friend, Judas, betray him with a kiss. Alas! poor Judas! He loved Jesus, in a way, like the rest did. It was only his fear of poverty that made him betray his Master. He was so poor – he wanted the money so badly! We cry out in horror against Judas. Let us pray rather that we are never tempted to do a shameful action for a few pieces of silver. The fear of poverty ever did, and ever will, make scamps of men. We would like to be faithful, and noble, and just, only really times are so bad that we cannot afford it! As Becky Sharp says, it is so easy to be good and noble on five thousand a year, so very hard if it be on the mere five. If Judas had only been a well-to-do man, he might have been Saint Judas this day, instead of cursed Judas. He was not bad. He had only one failing – the failing that makes the difference between a saint and a villain, all the world over – he was a coward; he was afraid of being poor.

'They saw him, pale and silent, dragged now before the priests of his own countrymen, and now before the Roman Governor, while the voice of the people – the people who had cried "Hosanna" to him – shouted "Crucify him! crucify him!" They saw him bleeding from the crown of thorns. They saw him, still followed by the barking mob, sink beneath the burden of his cross. They saw the woman wipe the bloody sweat from off his face. They saw the last, long, silent look between the mother and the son, as, journeying upward to his death, he passed her in the narrow way through which he once had ridden in brief-lived triumph. They heard her low sob as she turned away, leaning on Mary Magdalen. They saw him nailed upon the cross between the thieves. They saw the blood start from his side. They heard his last cry to his God. They saw him rise victorious over death!

'Few believing Christians among the vast audience but must have passed out from that strange playhouse with their belief and love strengthened. The God of the Christian, for his sake, became a man, and lived and suffered and died as a man; and, as a man, living, suffering, dying among other men, he had that day seen him.

'The unbeliever, also, passes out into the village street full of food for thought. The rude sermon preached in this hillside temple has shown to him, clearer than he could have seen before, the secret wherein lies the strength of Christianity; the reason why, of all the faiths that Nature has taught to her children to help them in their need, to satisfy the hunger of their souls, this faith, born by the Sea of Galilee, has spread the farthest over the world, and struck its note the deepest into human life. Not by his doctrines, not even by his promises, has Christ laid hold upon the hearts of men, but by the story of his life.'

(Diary of a Pilgrimage.)

SEE ENGLAND FIRST

To tell the truth, it was the journey more than the play that tempted me. To be a great traveller has always been one of my cherished ambitions. I yearn to be able to write in this sort of strain:

'I have smoked my fragant Havana in the sunny streets of old Madrid, and I have puffed the rude and not sweet-smelling calumet of peace in the draughty wigwam of the Wild West; I have sipped my evening coffee in the silent tent, while the tethered camel browsed without upon the desert grass, and I have quaffed the fiery brandy of the North while the reindeer munched his fodder beside me in the hut, and the pale light of the midnight sun threw the shadows of the pines across the snow; I have felt the stab of lustrous eyes that, ghostlike, looked at me from out veil-covered faces in Byzantium's narrow ways, and I have laughed back (though it was wrong of me to do so) at the saucy, wanton glances of the black-eyed girls of Jedo; I have wandered where "good" – but not too good – Haroun Alraschid crept disguised at nightfall, with his faithful Mesrour by his side; I have stood upon the bridge where Dante watched the sainted Beatrice pass by; I have floated on the waters that once bore the barge of Cleopatra; I have stood where Caesar fell; I have heard the soft rustle of rich, rare robes in the drawing-rooms of Mayfair, and I have heard the teeth-necklaces rattle around the ebony throats of the belles of Tongataboo; I have panted beneath the sun's fierce rays in India, and frozen under the icy blasts of Greenland; I have mingled with the teeming hordes of old Cathay, and, deep in the great pine forests of the Western World, I have lain, wrapped in my blanket, a thousand miles beyond the shores of human life.'

B., to whom I explained my learning towards this style of diction, said that exactly the same effect could be produced by writing about places quite handy. He said:

'I could go on like that without having been outside England at all. I should say:

'"I have smoked my fourpenny shag in the sanded bars of Fleet Street, and I have puffed my twopenny Manilla in the gilded halls of the Criterion; I have quaffed my foaming beer of Burton where Islington's famed Angel gathers the little thirsty ones beneath her shadowing wings, and I have sipped my tenpenny *ordinaire* in many a garlic-scented *salon* of Soho. On the back of the strangely-moving ass I have urged – or, to speak more correctly, the proprietor of the ass, or his agent, from behind has urged – my wild career across the sandy heaths of Hampstead, and my canoe has startled the screaming wild-fowl from their lonely haunts amid the sub-tropical regions of Battersea. Adown the long, steep slope of One Tree Hill have I rolled from top to foot, while laughing maidens of the East stood round and clapped their hands and yelled; and, in the old-world garden of that pleasant Court, where played the fair-haired children of the ill-starred Stuarts, have I wandered long through mazy paths, my arm entwined about the waist of one of Eve's sweet daughters, while her mother raged around indignantly on the other side of the hedge, and never seemed to get any nearer to us. I have chased the lodging-house Norfolk Howard to his watery death by the pale lamp's light; I have, shivering, followed the leaping flea o'er many a mile of pillow and sheet, by the great Atlantic's margin. Round and round, till the heart – and not only the heart – grows sick, and the mad brain whirls and reels, have I ridden the small, but extremely hard, horse, that may, for a penny, be mounted amid the plains of Peckham Rye; and high above the heads of the giddy throngs of Barnet (though it is doubtful if anyone among them was half so giddy as was I) have I swung in highly-coloured car, worked by a man with a rope. I have trod in stately measure the floor of Kensington's Town Hall (the tickets were a guinea each, and included refreshments – when you could get to them through the crowd), and on the green sward of the forest that borders eastern Anglia by the oft-sung town of Epping I have performed quaint ceremonies in a ring; I have mingled with the teeming hordes of Drury Lane on Boxing Night, and, during the run of a high-class piece, I have sat in lonely grandeur in the front row of the gallery, and wished that I had spent my shilling instead in the Oriental halls of the Alhambra."

'There you are,' said B., 'that is just as good as yours; and you can write like that without going more than a few hours' journey from London.'

(Diary of a Pilgrimage.)

AN EVENING AT THE PLAY

But the most marvellous feat, to my thinking, ever accomplished by Barbara was the bearing off of my father and mother to witness 'A Voice from the Grave, or the Power of Love. New and Original Drama in five acts and thirteen tableaux'.

They had been bred in a narrow creed, both my father and my mother. That Puritan blood flowed in their veins that throughout our land has drowned much harmless joyousness; yet those who know of it only from hearsay do foolishly to speak ill of it. If ever earnest times should come again, not how to enjoy but how to live being the question, Fate demanding of us to show not what we have, but what we are, we may regret that they are fewer among us than formerly, those who trained themselves to despise all pleasure, because in pleasure they saw the subtlest foe to principle and duty. No graceful growth, this Puritanism, for its roots are in the hard, stern facts of life; but it is strong, and from it has sprung all that is worth preserving in the Anglo-Saxon character. Its men feared and its women loved God, and if their words were harsh their hearts were tender. If they shut out the sunshine from their lives, it was that their eyes might see better the glory lying beyond; and if their view be correct, that earth's threescore years and ten are but a preparation for eternity, then who shall call them even foolish for turning away their thoughts from its allurements?

'Still, I think I should like to have a look at one, just to see what it is like,' argued my father; 'one cannot judge of a thing that one knows nothing about.'

I imagine that it was his first argument rather than his second that convinced my mother.

'That is true,' she answered. 'I remember how shocked my poor father was when he found me one night at the bedroom window reading Sir Walter Scott by the light of the moon.'

'What about the boy?' said my father, for I had been included in the invitation.

'We will all be wicked together,' said my mother.

So an evening or two later the four of us stood at the corner of Pigott Street waiting for the 'bus.

'It is a close evening,' said my father, 'let's go the whole hog and ride outside.'

In those days for a lady to ride outside a 'bus was as in these days for a lady to smoke in public. Surely my mother's guardian angel must have betaken himself off in a huff.

'Will you keep close behind and see to my skirt?' answered my mother, commencing preparations. If you will remember that these were the days of crinolines, that the 'knife-boards' of omnibuses were then approached by a perpendicular ladder, the rungs two feet apart, you will understand the necessity for such precaution.

Which of us was the most excited throughout that long ride it would be difficult to say. Barbara, feeling keenly her responsibility as prompter and leader of the dread enterprise, sat anxious, as she explained to us afterwards, hoping there would be nothing shocking in the play, nothing to belie its innocent title; pleased with her success so far, yet still fearful of failure, doubtful till the last moment lest we should suddenly repent, and stopping the 'bus, flee from the wrath to come. My father was the youngest of us all. Compared with him I was sober and contained. He fidgeted – people marked upon it. He hummed. But for the stern eye of a thin young man sitting next to him trying to read a paper, I believe he would have broken out into song. Every minute he would lean across to inquire of my mother: 'How are you feeling – all right?' To which my mother would reply with a nod and a smile. She sat very silent herself, clasping and unclasping her hands. As for myself, I remember feeling so sorry for the crowds that passed us on their way home. It was sad to think of the long, dull evening that lay before them. I wondered how they could face it.

Our seats were in the front row of the upper circle. The lights were low and the house only half full when we reached them.

'It seems very orderly and – and respectable,' whispered my mother. There seemed a touch of disappointment in her tone.

'We are rather early,' replied Barbara; 'it will be livelier when the band comes in and they turn up the gas.'

But even when this happened my mother was not content. 'There is so little room for the actors,' she complained.

It was explained to her that the green curtain would go up, that the stage lay behind.

So we waited, my mother sitting stiffly on the extreme edge of her seat, holding me tightly by the hand; I believe with some vague idea of flight, should out of that vault-scented gloom the devil suddenly appear to claim us for his own. But before the curtain was quite up she had forgotten him.

You poor folk that go to the theatre a dozen times a year, perhaps oftener, what do you know of plays? You see no drama, you see but middle-aged Mr Brown, churchwarden, payer of taxes, foolishly pretending to be a brigand; Miss Jones, daughter of old Jones, the chemist, making believe to be a haughty princess. How can you, a grown man, waste money on a seat to witness such tomfoolery? What we saw was something very different. A young and beautiful girl – true, not a lady by birth, being merely the daughter of an honest yeoman, but one equal in all the essentials of womanhood to the noblest in the land – suffered before our very eyes an amount of misfortune that, had one not seen it for oneself, one could never have believed Fate could have accumulated upon the head of any single individual. Beside her woes our own poor troubles sank into insignificance. We had used to grieve, as my mother in a whisper reminded my father, if now and again we had not been able to afford meat for dinner. This poor creature, driven from her wretched attic, compelled to wander through the snow without so much as an umbrella to protect her, had not even a crust to eat; and yet never lost her faith in Providence. It was a lesson, as my mother remarked afterwards, that she would never forget. And virtue had been triumphant, let shallow critics say what they will. Had we not proved it with our own senses? The villain – I think his Christian name, if one can apply the word 'Christian' in connection with such a fiend, was Jasper – had never really loved the heroine. He was incapable of love. My mother had felt this before he had been on the stage five minutes, and my father – in spite of protests from callous people behind who appeared to be utterly indifferent to what was going on under their very noses – had agreed with her. What he was in love with was her fortune – the fortune that had been left to her by her uncle in Australia, but about which nobody but the villain knew anything. Had she swerved a hair's breadth from the course of almost supernatural rectitude, had her love for the hero ever weakened, her belief in him – in spite of damning evidence to the contrary – for a moment wavered, then wickedness might have triumphed. How at times, knowing all the facts but helpless to interfere, we trembled, lest, deceived by the cruel lies the villain told her, she should yield to importunity! How we thrilled when, in language eloquent though rude, she flung his false love back into his teeth! Yet still we feared. We knew well that it was not the hero who had done the murder. 'Poor dear,' as Amy would have called him, he was quite incapable of doing anything requiring one-half as much smartness. We knew that it was not he, poor innocent lamb! who had betrayed the lady with the French accent; we had heard her on the subject, and had formed a very shrewd conjecture. But appearances, we could not help admitting, were terribly to his disfavour. The circumstantial evidence against him would have hanged an archbishop. Could she in face of it still retain her faith? There were moments when my mother restrained with difficulty her desire to rise and explain.

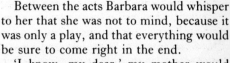

Between the acts Barbara would whisper to her that she was not to mind, because it was only a play, and that everything would be sure to come right in the end.

'I know, my dear,' my mother would answer, laughing, 'it is very foolish of me; I forget. Paul, when you see me getting excited, you must remind me.'

But of what use was I in such case? I, who only by holding on to the arms of my seat could keep myself from swarming down on to the stage to fling myself between this noble damsel and her perse- cutor – this fair-haired, creamy angel, in whose presence for the time being I had forgotten even Barbara?

The end came at last. The uncle from Australia was not dead. The villain – bungler as well as knave – had killed the wrong man – somebody of no importance whatever. As a matter of fact, the comic man himself was the uncle from Australia – had been so all along. My mother had had a suspicion of this from the very first. She told us so three times – to make up, I suppose, for not having mentioned it before. How we cheered and laughed, in spite of the tears in our eyes!

By pure accident it happened to be the first night of the piece, and the author, in response to much shouting and whistling, came before the curtain. He was fat, and looked commonplace, but I deemed him a genius, and my mother said he had a good face, and waved her handkerchief wildly, while my father shouted 'Bravo!' long after everybody else had finished; and people round about muttered 'Packed house',

104

which I didn't understand at the time, but came to later.

And stranger still, it happened to be before that very same curtain that many years later I myself stepped forth to make my first bow as a playwright. I saw the house but dimly, for on such occasion one's vision is apt to be clouded. All that I clearly saw was in the front row of the second circle – a sweet face laughing, though the tears were in her eyes; and she waved to me a handkerchief. And on one side of her stood a gallant gentleman with merry eyes, who shouted 'Bravo!' and on the other a dreamy-looking lad, but he appeared disappointed, having expected better work from me. And the fourth face I could not see, for it was turned away from me.

Barbara, determined on completeness, insisted upon supper. In those days respectability fed at home, but one resort possible there was: an eating-house with some pretence to gaiety behind St Clement Danes, and to that she led us. It was a long, narrow room, divided into wooden compartments after the old coffee-house plan, a gangway down the centre. Now we should call it a dismal hole, and closing the door, hasten away. But to Adam, Eve in her Sunday fig-leaves was a stylishly dressed

The villain – bungler as well as knave – had killed the wrong man.

woman; and to my eyes, with its gilded mirrors and its flaring gas, the place seemed a palace.

Barbara ordered oysters, a fish that familiarity with its empty shell had made me curious concerning. Truly, no spot on the globe is so rich in oyster shells as the East End of London. A stranger might be led to the impression (erroneous) that the customary lunch of the East End labourer consisted of oysters. How they collect there in such quantities is a mystery, though Washburn, to whom I once presented the problem, found no difficulty in solving it to his own satisfaction: 'To the rich man the oyster; to the poor man the shell. Thus are the Creator's gifts divided among all His creatures, none being sent empty away.' For drink the others had stout, and I had ginger beer. The waiter, who called me 'Sir', advised against this mixture, but among us all the dominating sentiment by this time was that nothing really mattered very much. Afterwards my father called for a cigar and boldly lighted it, though my mother looked anxious, and fortunately, perhaps, it would not draw. And then it came out that he himself had once written a play.

'You never told me of that,' complained my mother.

'It was a long while ago,' replied my father; 'nothing came of it.'

'It might have been a success,' said my mother; 'you always had a gift for writing.'

'I must look it over again,' said my father. 'I had quite forgotten it, I have an impression it wasn't at all bad.'

'It can be of much help,' said my mother, 'a good play; it makes one think.'

We put Barbara into a cab, and rode home ourselves inside a 'bus. My mother was tired, so my father slipped his arm round her, telling her to lean against him, and soon she fell asleep with her head upon his shoulder. A coarse-looking wench sat opposite, her man's arm round her likewise, and she also fell asleep, her powdered face against his coat.

'They can do with a bit of nursing, can't they?' said the man, with a grin, to the conductor.

'Ah, they're just kids,' agreed the conductor sympathetically, 'that's what they are, all of 'em, just kids.'

(Paul Kelver.)

HIS FIRST ENGAGEMENT

A delightful dreaminess was stealing over me. Everything and everybody appeared to be a long way off, but, whether because of this or in spite of it, exceedingly attractive. Never had I noticed the Signora so bewitching; in a motherly sort of way even the third-floor front was good to look upon; Mrs Peedles I could almost have believed to be the real Flora MacDonald sitting in front of me. But the vision of Miss Rosina Sellars made literally my head to swim. Never before had I dared to cast upon female loveliness the satisfying gaze with which I now boldly regarded her every movement. Evidently she noticed it, for she turned away her eyes. I had heard that exceptionally strong-minded people merely by concentrating their will could make other ordinary people do just whatever they, the exceptionally strong-minded people, wished. I willed that Miss Rosina Sellars should turn her eyes again towards me. Victory crowned my efforts. Evidently I was one of these exceptionally strong-minded persons. Slowly her eyes came round and met mine with a smile – a helpless, pathetic smile that said, so I read it: 'You know no woman can resist you: be merciful!'

Inflamed by the brutal lust of conquest I suppose I must have willed still further, for the next thing I remember is sitting with Miss Sellars on the sofa, holding her hand, the while the O'Kelly sang a sentimental ballad, only one line of which comes back to me! 'For the angels must have told him, and he knows I love him now,' much stress upon the 'now.' The others had their backs towards us. Miss Sellars, with a look that pierced my heart, dropped her somewhat large head upon my shoulder, leaving, as I observed the next day, a patch of powder on my coat.

Miss Sellars observed that one of the saddest things in the world was unrequited love.

I replied gallantly, 'Whateryou know about it?'

'Ah, you men, you men,' murmured Miss Sellars; 'you're all alike.'

This suggested a personal aspersion on my character. 'Not allerus,' I murmured.

'You don't know what love is,' said Miss Sellars. 'You're not old enough.'

The O'Kelly had passed on to Sullivan's 'Sweethearts,' then in its first popularity.

> 'Oh, love for a year – a week – a day!
> But oh for the love that loves al-wa-ay!'

Miss Sellars' languishing eyes were fixed upon me; Miss Sellars' red lips pouted and twitched; Miss Sellars' white bosom rose and fell. Never, so it seemed to me, had so large an amount of beauty been concentrated in one being.

'Yeserdo,' I said. 'I love you.'

I stooped to kiss the red lips, but something was in my way. It turned out to be a cold cigar. Miss Sellars thoughtfully removed it, and threw it away. Our lips met. Her large arms closed about my neck and held me tight.

'Well, I'm sure!' came the voice of Mrs Peedles, as from afar. 'Nice goings-on!'

I have vague remembrance of a somewhat heated discussion in which everybody but myself appeared to be taking extreme interest – of Miss Sellars in her most ladylike and chilling tones defending me against the charge of 'being no gentleman', which Mrs Peedles was explaining nobody had said I wasn't. The argument seemed to be of the circular order. No gentleman had ever kissed Miss Sellars who had not every right to do so, nor ever would. To kiss Miss Sellars without such right was to declare himself no gentleman. Miss Sellars appealed to me to clear my character from the aspersion of being no gentleman. I was trying to understand the situation when Jarman, seizing me somewhat roughly by the arm, suggested my going to bed. Miss Sellars, seizing my other arm, suggested my refusing to go to bed. So far I was with Miss Sellars – I didn't want to go to bed and said so. My desire to sit up longer was proof positive to Miss Sellars that I was a gentleman, but to no one else. The argument shifted, the question being now as to whether Miss Sellars were a lady. To prove the point it was, according to Miss Sellars, necessary that I should repeat I loved her. I did repeat it, adding, with a faint remembrance of my own fiction, that if a life's devotion was likely to be of the slightest further proof, my heart's blood was at her service. This cleared the air, Mrs Peedles observing that under such circumstances it only remained for her to withdraw everything she had said; to which Miss Sellars replied graciously that she had always known Mrs Peedles to be a good sort at bottom.

Nevertheless, gaiety was gone from among us, and for this, in some way I could not understand, I appeared to be responsible. Jarman was distinctly sulky. The O'Kelly, suddenly thinking of the time, went to the door and discovered that the two cabs were waiting. The third floor recollected that work had to be finished. I myself felt sleepy.

Our host and hostess departed, Jarman again suggested bed, and this time I agreed with him. After a slight misunderstanding with the door, I found myself upon the stairs. I had never noticed before that they were quite perpendicular. Adapting myself to the changed conditions, I climbed them with the help of my hands. I accomplished the last flight somewhat quickly, and feeling tired, sat down the moment I was within my room. Jarman knocked at the door. I told him to come in; but he didn't. It occurred to me that the reason was I was sitting on the floor with my back against the door. The discovery amused me exceedingly, and I laughed; and Jarman, baffled, descended to his own floor. I found getting into bed a difficulty owing to the strange behaviour of the room. It spun round and round. Now the bed was just in front of me, now it was behind me. I managed at last to catch it before it could get past me, and holding on by the ironwork, frustrated its efforts to throw me out again on to the floor.

But it was some time before I went to sleep, and over my intervening experiences I draw a veil.

(Paul Kelver.)

I found getting into bed a difficulty owing to the strange behaviour of the room.

HUMOUR AND 'THE PENNY-A-LINER'

To my literary labours I found it necessary to add journalism.
I lacked Dan's magnificent assurance. Fate never befriends the
nervous. Had I burst into the editorial sanctum, the editor
most surely would have been out; if in, would have been a man
of short ways, would have seen to it that I went out, quickly.
But the idea was not to be thought of; Robert Macaire himself
in my one coat would have been diffident, apologetic. I joined
the ranks of the penny-a-liners – to be literally exact, three-
halfpence-a-liners. In company with half-a-dozen other shabby
outsiders – some of them young men like myself seeking to
climb; others, old men who had sunk – I attended inquests,
police courts; flew after fire-engines; rejoiced in street-
accidents; yearned for murders. Somewhat vulture-like we
lived precariously upon the misfortunes of others. We made
occasional half-crowns by providing the public with scandal,
occasional crowns by keeping our information to ourselves.

'I think, gentlemen,' would explain our spokesman in a
hoarse whisper, on returning to the table, 'I think the corpse's
brother-in-law is anxious that the affair, if possible, should be
kept out of the papers.'

The closeness and attention with which we would follow
that particular case, the fulness and completeness of our notes,
would be quite remarkable. Our spokesman would rise, drift
carelessly away, to return five minutes later, wiping his mouth.

'Not a very interesting case, gentlemen, I don't think. Shall
we say five shillings apiece?' Sometimes a sense of the dignity
of our calling would induce us to stand out for ten.

And here also my sense of humour came to my aid; gave me

112

perhaps an undue advantage over my competitors. Twelve good men and true had been asked to say how a Lascar sailor had met his death. It was perfectly clear how he had met his death. A plumber, working on the roof of a small two-storied house, had slipped and fallen on him. The plumber had escaped with a few bruises; the unfortunate sailor had been picked up dead. Some blame attached to the plumber. His mate, an excellent witness, told us the whole story.

'I was fixing a gas-pipe on the first floor,' said the man. 'The prisoner was on the roof.'

'We won't call him the "prisoner,"' interrupted the coroner, 'at least, not yet. Refer to him, if you please, as the "last witness."'

'The last witness,' corrected himself the man. 'He shouts down the chimney to know if I was ready for him.'

Others, old men who had sunk.

'"Ready and waiting," I says.

'"Right," he says; "I'm coming in through the window."

'"Wait a bit," I says; "I'll go down and move the ladder for you."

'"It's all right," he says; "I can reach it."

'"No, you can't," I says. "It's the other side of the chimney."

'"I can get round," he says.

'Well, before I knew what had happened, I hears him go, smack! I rushes to the window and looks out; I see him on the pavement, sitting up like.

'"Hullo, Jim," I says. "Have you hurt yourself?"

'"I think I'm all right," he says, "as far as I can tell. But I wish you'd come down. This bloke I've fallen on looks a bit sick."'

The others headed their flimsy 'Sad Accident', a title truthful but not alluring. I altered mine to 'Plumber in a Hurry – Fatal Result'. Saying as little as possible about the unfortunate sailor, I called the attention of plumbers generally to the coroner's very just remarks upon the folly of undue haste; pointed out to them, as a body, the trouble that would arise if somehow they could not cure themselves of this tendency to rush through their work without a moment's loss of time.

It established for me a useful reputation. The sub-editor of one evening paper condescended so far as to come out in his shirt-sleeves and shake hands with me.

'That's the sort of thing we want,' he told me; 'a light touch, a bit of humour.'

I snatched fun from fires (I sincerely trust the insurance premiums were not overdue); culled quaintness from street rows; extracted merriment from catastrophes the most painful, and prospered.

(Paul Kelver.)

THE PRINCESS SENDS PAUL A RING

It was an evening in Brussels. Strolling idly after dinner, the bright lights of a theatre invited me to enter. It was somewhat late; the second act had commenced. I slipped quietly into my seat, the only one vacant at the extreme end of the front row of the first *rang;* then looking down upon the stage, met her eyes. A little later an attendant whispered to me that Madame G——would like to see me; so at the fall of the curtain I went round. Two men were in the dressing-room smoking, and on the table were some bottles of champagne. She was standing before her glass, a loose shawl about her shoulders.

'Excuse my shaking hands,' she said. 'This damned hole is like a furnace; I have to make up fresh after each act.'

She held them out for my inspection with a laugh; they were smeared with grease.

'D'you know my husband?' she continued. 'Baron G——; Mr Paul Kelver.'

The Baron rose. He was a red-faced, pot-bellied little man. 'Delighted to meet Mr Kelver,' he said, speaking in excellent English. 'Any friend of my wife's is always a friend of mine.'

He held out his fat, perspiring hand. I was not in the mood to attach much importance to ceremony. I bowed and turned away, careless whether he was offended or not.

'I am glad I saw you,' she continued. 'Do you remember a girl called Barbara? You and she were rather chums, years ago.'

'Yes,' I answered, 'I remember her.'

'Well, she died, poor girl, three years ago.' She was rubbing paint into her cheeks as she spoke. 'She asked me if ever I saw you to give you this. I have been carrying it about with me ever since.'

She took a ring from her finger. It was the one ring Barbara had worn as a girl, a chrysolite set plainly in a band of gold. I had noticed it upon her hand the first time I had seen her, sitting in my father's office framed by the dusty books and papers. She dropped it into my outstretched palm.

'Quite a pretty little romance,' laughed the Baron.

'That's all,' added the woman at the glass. 'She said you would understand.'

'Quite a pretty little romance,' laughed the Baron.

From under her painted lashes she flashed a glance at me. I hope never to see again that look upon a woman's face.

'Thank you,' I said. 'Yes, I understand. It was very kind of you. I shall always wear it.'

Placing the ring upon my finger, I left the room.

(Paul Kelver.)

HOW TO WRITE A PLAY

I had written a few farces, comediettas, and they had been successful. But the chief piece of the evening is a serious responsibility. A young man may be excused for hesitating. It can make, but also it can mar him. A comic opera above all other forms of art – if I may be forgiven for using the sacred word in connection with such a subject – demands experience.

I explained my fears. I did not explain that in my desk lay a four-act drama throbbing with humanity, with life, with which it had been my hope – growing each day fainter – to take the theatrical public by storm, to establish myself as a serious playwright.

'It's very simple,' urged Hodgson. 'Provide A—— plenty of comic business; you ought to be able to do that all right. Give G—— something pretty in waltz time, and D—— a part in which she can change her frock every quarter of an hour or so, and the thing is done.

'I'll tell you what,' continued Hodgson. 'I'll take the whole crowd down to Richmond on Sunday. We'll have a coach, and leave the theatre at half-past ten. It will be an opportunity for you to study them. You'll be able to have a talk with them and get to know just what they can do. A—— has ideas in his head; he'll explain them to you. Then, next week, we'll draw up a contract and set to work.'

It was too good an opportunity to let slip, though I knew that if successful I should find myself pinned down firmer than ever to my rôle of jester. But it is remunerative, the writing of comic opera.

A small crowd had gathered in the Strand to see us start.

'Nothing wrong, is there?' inquired the leading lady, in a tone of some anxiety, alighting a quarter of an hour late from her cab. 'It isn't a fire, is it?'

'Merely assembled to see you,' explained Mr Hodgson, without raising his eyes from his letters.

'Oh, good gracious!' cries the leading lady, 'do let us get away quickly.'

'Box seat, my dear,' returned Mr Hodgson.

The leading lady, accepting the proffered assistance of myself and three other gentlemen, mounted the ladder with charming hesitation. Some delay in getting off was caused by our low comedian, who twice, making believe to miss his footing, slid down again into the arms of the stolid doorkeeper. The crowd, composed for the most part of small boys, approving the endeavour to amuse them, laughed and applauded. Our low comedian, thus encouraged, made a third attempt upon his hands and knees, and, gaining the roof, sat down upon the tenor, who smiled somewhat mechanically.

The first dozen or so 'buses we passed, our low comedian greeted by rising to his feet and bowing profoundly, afterwards falling back upon either the tenor or myself. Except by the tenor and myself his performance appeared to be much appreciated. Charing Cross passed, and nobody seeming to be interested in our progress, to the relief of the tenor and myself, he settled down.

'People sometimes ask me,' said the low comedian, brushing the dust off his knees, 'why I do this sort of thing off the stage. It amuses me.'

'I was coming up to London the other day from Birmingham,' he continued. 'At Willesden, when the ticket collector opened the door, I sprang out of the carriage and ran off down the platform. Of course, he ran after me, shouting to all the others to stop me. I dodged them for about a minute. You wouldn't believe the excitement there was. Quite fifty people left their seats to see what it was all about. I explained to them

He attracted a certain amount of attention by balancing the horn upon his nose.

when they caught me that I had been travelling second with a first-class ticket, which was the fact. People think I do it to attract attention. I do it for my own pleasure.'

'It must be a trouble-some way of amusing oneself,' I suggested.

'Exactly what my wife says,' he replied; 'she can never understand the desire that comes over us all, I suppose, at times, to play the fool. As a rule, when she is with me I don't do it.'

'She is not here to-day?' I asked, glancing round.

'She suffers from headaches,' he answered, 'she hardly ever goes anywhere.'

'I'm sorry.' I spoke not out of mere politeness; I really did feel sorry.

During the drive to Richmond this irrepressible desire to amuse himself got the better of him more than once or twice. Through Kensington he attracted a certain amount of attention by balancing the horn upon his nose. At Kew he stopped the coach to request of a young ladies' boarding school change

for sixpence. At the foot of Richmond Hill he caused a crowd
to assemble while trying to persuade a deaf old gentleman in a
Bath-chair to allow his man to race us up the hill for a shilling.

At these antics and such-like our party laughed uproariously,
with the exception of Hodgson, who had his correspondence to
attend to, and an elegant young lady of some social standing who
had lately emerged from the divorce court with a reputation
worth to her in cash a hundred pounds a week.

Arriving at the hotel, a quarter of an hour or so before lunch
time, we strolled into the garden. Our low comedian, observing an elderly gentleman of dignified appearance sipping a
glass of Vermouth at a small table, stood for a moment rooted
to the earth with astonishment, then, making a bee-line for the
stranger, seized and shook him warmly by the hand. We
exchanged admiring glances with one another.

'Charlie is in good form to-day,' we told one another, and
followed at his heels.

The elderly gentleman had risen; he looked puzzled.

'And how's Aunt Martha?' asked him our low comedian.
'Dear old Aunt Martha! Well, I am glad! You do look bonny!
How is she?'

'I'm afraid——' commenced the elderly gentleman.

Our low comedian started back. Other visitors had gathered
round.

'Don't tell me anything has happened to her! Not dead?
Don't tell me that!'

He seized the bewildered gentleman by the shoulders and
presented him a face distorted by terror.

'I really have not the faintest notion what you are talking
about,' returned the gentleman, who seemed annoyed. 'I don't
know you.'

'Not know me? Do you mean to tell me you've forgotten——?
Isn't your name Steggles?'

'No, it isn't,' returned the stranger somewhat shortly.

'My mistake,' replied our low comedian. He tossed off at one gulp what remained of the stranger's Vermouth and walked away rapidly.

The elderly gentleman, not seeing the humour of the joke, one of our party to soothe him explained to him that it was A——, *the* A——, – Charlie A——.

'Oh, is it?' growled the elderly gentleman. 'Then will you tell him from me that when I want his damned tomfoolery I'll come to the theatre and pay for it.'

'What a disagreeable man!' we said, as, following our low comedian, we made our way into the hotel.

During lunch he continued in excellent spirits; kissed the bald back of the waiter's head, pretending to mistake it for a face, called for hot mustard and water, made believe to steal the silver, and when the finger bowls arrived, took off his coat and requested the ladies to look the other way.

After lunch he became suddenly serious, and slipping his arm through mine, led me by unfrequented paths.

'Now, about this new opera,' he said; 'we don't want any of the old stale business. Give us something new.'

I suggested that to do so might be difficult.

'Not at all,' he answered. 'Now my idea is this. I am a young fellow, and I'm in love with a girl.'

I promised to make a note of it.

'Her father, apoplectic old idiot – make him comic; "Damme, sir! By gad!" all that sort of thing.'

By persuading him that I understood what he meant, I rose in his estimation.

'He won't have anything to say to me – thinks I'm an ass. I'm a simple sort of fellow – on the outside. But I'm not such a fool as I look.'

'You don't think we are getting too much out of the groove?' I inquired.

His opinion was that the more so the better.

'Very well. Then, in the second act I disguise myself. I'll come on as an organ grinder, sing a song in broken English, then as a policeman, or a young swell about town. Give me plenty of opportunity, that's the great thing – opportunity to be really funny, I mean. We don't want any of the old stale tricks.'

I promised him my support.

'Put a little pathos in it,' he added; 'give me a scene where I can show them I've something else in me besides merely humour. We don't want to make them howl, but just to feel a little. Let's send them out of the theatre saying, "Well, Charlie's often made me laugh, but I'm damned if I knew he could make me cry before!" See what I mean?'

I told him I thought I did.

The leading lady, meeting us on our return, requested, with pretty tone of authority, everybody else to go away and leave us. There were cries of 'Naughty!' The leading lady, laughing girlishly, took me by the hand and ran away with me.

'I want to talk to you,' said the leading lady, as soon as we had reached a secluded seat overlooking the river, 'about my part in the new opera. Now, can't you give me something original? Do.'

Her pleading was so pretty, there was nothing for it but to pledge compliance.

'I am so tired of being the simple village maiden,' said the leading lady; 'what I want is a part with some opportunity in it – a coquettish part. I can flirt,' assured me the leading lady archly. 'Try me.'

I satisfied her of my perfect faith.

'You might,' said the leading lady, 'see your way to making the plot depend upon me. It always seems to me that the woman's part is never made enough of in comic opera. I am sure a comic opera built round a woman would be a really great success. Don't you agree with me, Mr Kelver?' pouted the leading lady, laying her pretty hand on mine. 'We are much more interesting than the men – now, aren't we?'

Personally, as I told her, I agreed with her.

The tenor, sipping tea with me on the balcony, beckoned me aside.

'About this new opera,' said the tenor; 'doesn't it seem to you the time has come to make more of the story – that the public might prefer a little more human interest and a little less clowning?'

I admitted that a good plot was essential.

'It seems to me,' said the tenor, 'that if you could write an opera round an interesting love story, you would score a success. Of course, let there be plenty of humour, but reduce it to its proper place. As a support, it is excellent; when it is made the entire structure, it is apt to be tiresome – at least, that is my view.'

I replied with sincerity that there seemed to be much truth in what he said.

'Of course, so far as I am personally concerned,' went on the tenor, 'it is immaterial. I draw the same salary whether I'm on the stage five minutes or an hour. But when you have a man of my position in the cast, and give him next to nothing to do – well, the public are disappointed.'

'Most naturally,' I commented.

'The lover,' whispered the tenor, noticing the careless approach towards us of the low comedian, 'that's the character they are thinking about all the time – men and women both. It's human nature. Make your lover interesting – that's the secret.'

Waiting for the horses to be put to, I became aware of the fact that I was standing some distance from the others in company with a tall, thin, somewhat oldish-looking man. He spoke in low, hurried tones, fearful evidently of being over-heard and interrupted.

'You'll forgive me, Mr Kelver,' he said – 'Trevor, Marmaduke Trevor. I play the Duke of Bayswater in the second act.'

I was unable to recall him for the moment; there were quite a number of small parts in the second act. But glancing into his sensitive face, I shrank from wounding him.

'A capital performance,' I lied. 'It has always amused me.'

He flushed with pleasure. 'I made a great success some years ago,' he said, 'in America with a soda-water syphon, and it occurred to me that if you could, Mr Kelver, in a natural sort of way, drop in a small part leading up to a little business with a soda-water syphon, it might help the piece.'

I wrote him his soda-water scene, I am glad to remember, and insisted upon it, in spite of a good deal of opposition. Some of the critics found fault with the incident, as lacking in originality. But Marmaduke Trevor was quite right, it did help a little.

Our return journey was an exaggerated repetition of our morning drive. Our low comedian produced hideous noises from the horn, and entered into contests of running wit with 'bus-drivers – a decided mistake from his point of view, the score generally remaining with the 'bus-driver. At Hammersmith, seizing the opportunity of a block in the traffic, he assumed the rôle of cheap-jack, and standing up on the back seat, offered all our hats for sale at temptingly low prices.

'Got any ideas out of them?' asked Hodgson, when the time came for us to say good-night.

'I'm thinking, if you don't mind,' I answered, 'of going down into the country and writing the piece quietly, away from everybody.'

(Paul Kelver.)

MALVINA OF BRITTANY

It commenced, so I calculate, about the year 2000 B.C., or, to be more precise – for figures are not the strong point of the old chroniclers – when King Heremon ruled over Ireland and Harbundia was Queen of the White Ladies of Brittany, the fairy Malvina being her favourite attendant. It is with Malvina that this story is chiefly concerned. Various quite pleasant happenings are recorded to her credit. The White Ladies belonged to the 'good people,' and, on the whole, lived up to their reputation. But in Malvina, side by side with that is commendable, there appears to have existed a most reprehensible spirit of mischief, displaying itself in pranks that, excusable, or at all events understandable, in, say, a pixy or pigwidgeon, strike one as altogether unworthy of a well-principled White Lady, posing as the friend and benefactress of mankind. For merely refusing to dance with her – at midnight, by the shores of a mountain lake; neither the time nor the place calculated to appeal to an elderly gentleman, suffering possibly from rheumatism – she on one occasion transformed an eminently respectable proprietor of tin mines into a nightingale, necessitating a change of habits that to a business man must have been singularly irritating. On another occasion a quite important queen, having had the misfortune to quarrel with Malvina over some absurd point of etiquette in connection with a lizard, seems, on waking the next morning, to have found herself changed into what one judges, from the somewhat vague description afforded by the ancient chroniclers, to have been a sort of vegetable marrow.

Such changes, according to the Professor, who is prepared

to maintain that evidence of an historical nature exists sufficient to prove that the White Ladies formed at one time an
actual living community, must be taken in an allegorical sense.
Just as modern lunatics believe themselves to be china vases or
poll-parrots, and think and behave as such, so it must have
been easy, the Professor argues, for beings of superior intelligence to have exerted hypnotic influence upon the supersti-
tious savages by whom they were surrounded, and who,
intellectually considered, could have been little more than
children.

'Take Nebuchadnezzar.' I am still quoting the Professor.
'Nowadays we should put him into a strait-waistcoat. Had he
lived in Northern Europe instead of Southern Asia, legend
would have told us how some Kobold or Stromkarl had turned
him into a composite amalgamation of a serpent, a cat and a
kangaroo.' Be that as it may, this passion for change – in other
people – seems to have grown upon Malvina until she must
have become little short of a public nuisance, and eventually it
landed her in trouble.

The incident is unique in the annals of the White Ladies,
and the chroniclers dwell upon it with evident satisfaction. It
came about through the betrothal of King Heremon's only son,
Prince Gerbot, to the Princess Berchta of Normandy. Malvina
seems to have said nothing, but to have bided her time. The
White Ladies of Brittany, it must be remembered, were not
fairies pure and simple. Under certain conditions they were
capable of becoming women, and this fact, one takes it, must
have exerted a disturbing influence upon their relationships
with eligible male mortals. Prince Gerbot may not have been
altogether blameless. Young men in those sadly unenlightened
days may not, in their dealings with ladies, white or otherwise,
have always been the soul of discretion and propriety. One
would like to think the best of her.

But even the best is indefensible. On the day appointed for
the wedding she seems to have surpassed herself. Into what

particular shape or form she altered the wretched Prince Gerbot; or into what shape or form she persuaded him that he had been altered, it really, so far as the moral responsibility of Malvina is concerned, seems to be immaterial; the chronicle does not state; evidently something too indelicate for a self-respecting chronicler to even hint at. As, judging from other passages in the book, squeamishness does not seem to have been the author's literary failing, the sensitive reader can feel only grateful for the omission. It would have been altogether too harrowing.

It had, of course, from Malvina's point of view, the desired effect. The Princess Berchta appears to have given one look

The Princess Berchta appears to have fallen fainting into the arms of her attendants.

and then to have fallen fainting into the arms of her attendants. The marriage was postponed indefinitely, and Malvina, one sadly suspects, chortled. Her triumph was short-lived.

Unfortunately for her, King Heremon had always been a patron of the arts and science of his period. Among his friends were to be reckoned magicians, genii, the Nine Korrigans or Fays of Brittany – all sorts of parties capable of exerting influence, and, as events proved, only too willing. Ambassadors waited upon Queen Harbundia; and Harbundia, even had she wished, as on many previous occasions, to stand by her favourite, had no alternative. The fairy Malvina was called upon to return to Prince Gerbot his proper body and all therein contained.

She flatly refused. A self-willed, obstinate fairy, suffering from swelled head. And then there was that personal note. Merely that he should marry the Princess Berchta! She would see King Heremon, and Anniamus, in his silly old wizard's robe, and the Fays of Brittany, and all the rest of them——! A really nice White Lady may not have cared to finish the sentence, even to herself. One imagines the flash of the fairy eye, the stamp of the fairy foot. What could they do to her, any of them, with all their clacking of tongues and their wagging of heads? She, an immortal fairy! She would change Prince Gerbot back at a time of her own choosing. Let them attend to their own tricks and leave her to mind hers. One pictures long walks and talks between the distracted Harbundia and her refractory favourite – appeals to reason, to sentiment: 'For my sake.' 'Don't you see?' 'After all, dear, and even if he did.'

It seems to have ended by Harbundia losing all patience. One thing there was she could do that Malvina seems either not to have known of or not to have anticipated. A solemn meeting of the White Ladies was convened for the night of the midsummer moon. The place of meeting is described by the ancient chroniclers with more than their usual exactitude. It was on the land that the magician Kalyb had, ages ago, raised

128

up above all Brittany to form the grave of King Taramis. The 'Sea of the Seven Islands' lay to the north. One guesses it to be the ridge formed by the Arree Mountains. 'The Lady of the Fountain' appears to have been present, suggesting the deep green pool from which the river D'Argent takes its source. Roughly speaking, one would place it half-way between the modern towns of Morlaix and Callac. Pedestrians, even of the present day, speak of the still loneliness of that high plateau, treeless, houseless, with no sign of human hand there but that high, towering monolith round which the shrill winds moan incessantly. There, possibly on some broken fragment of these great grey stones, Queen Harbundia sat in judgment. And the judgment was – and from it there was no appeal – that the fairy Malvina should be cast out from among the community of the White Ladies of Brittany. Over the face of the earth she should wander, alone and unforgiven. Solemnly from the book of the roll-call of the White Ladies the name of Malvina was struck out for ever.

The blow must have fallen upon Malvina as heavily as it was unexpected. Without a word, without one backward look, she seems to have departed. One pictures the white, frozen face, the wide-open, unseeing eyes, the trembling, uncertain steps, the groping hands, the deathlike silence clinging like grave-clothes round about her.

From that night the fairy Malvina disappears from the book of the chroniclers of the White Ladies of Brittany, from legend and from folklore whatsoever. She does not appear again in history till the year A.D. 1914.

(Malvina of Brittany.)

THE FAWN GLOVES

Always he remembered her as he saw her first: the little spiritual face, the little brown shoes pointing downwards, their toes just touching the ground; the little fawn gloves folded upon her lap. He was not conscious of having noticed her with any particular attention: a plainly-dressed, childish-looking figure alone on a seat between him and the setting sun. Even had he felt curious his shyness would have prevented his deliberately running the risk of meeting her eyes. Yet immediately he had passed her he saw her again, quite clearly: the pale oval face, the brown shoes, and, between them, the little fawn gloves folded one over the other. All down the Broad Walk and across Primrose Hill, he saw her silhouetted against the sinking sun. At least that much of her: the wistful face and the trim brown shoes and the little folded hands; until the sun went down behind the high chimneys of the brewery beyond Swiss Cottage, and then she faded.

She was there again the next evening, precisely in the same place. Usually he walked home by the Hampstead Road. Only occasionally, when the beauty of the evening tempted him, would he take the longer way by Regent Street and through the Park. But so often it made him feel sad, the quiet Park, forcing upon him the sense of his own loneliness.

He would walk down merely as far as the Great Vase, so he arranged with himself. If she were not there – it was not likely that she would be – he would turn back into Albany Street. The newsvendors' shops with their display of the cheaper illustrated papers, the second-hand furniture dealers with their faded engravings and old prints, would give him something to look at, to take away his thoughts from himself. But seeing her in the distance, almost the moment he had entered the gate, it came to him how disappointed he would have been had the seat in front of the red tulip bed been vacant. A little away from her he paused, turning to look at the flowers. He thought that, waiting his opportunity, he might be able to steal a glance at her undetected. Once for a moment he did so, but venturing a second time their eyes met, or he fancied they did, and blushing furiously he hurried past. But again she came with him, or, rather, preceded him. On each empty seat between him and the sinking sun he saw her quite plainly: the pale oval face and the brown shoes, and, between them, the fawn gloves folded one upon the other.

Only this evening, about the small, sensitive mouth there seemed to be hovering just the faintest suggestion of a timid smile. And this time she lingered with him past Queen's Crescent and the Malden Road, till he turned into Carlton Street. It was dark in the passage, and he had to grope his way up the stairs, but with his hand on the door of the bed-sitting room on the third floor he felt less afraid of the solitude that would rise to meet him.

All day long in the dingy back office in Abingdon Street, Westminster, where from ten to six each day he sat copying briefs and petitions, he thought over what he would say to her; tactful beginnings by means of which he would slide into conversation with her. Up Portland Place he would rehearse them to himself. But at Cambridge Gate, when the little fawn gloves came in view, the words would run away, to join him again maybe at the gate into the Chester Road, leaving him meanwhile to pass her with stiff, hurried steps and eyes fixed straight in front of him. And so it might have continued, but that one evening she was no longer at her usual seat. A crowd of noisy children swarmed over it, and suddenly it seemed to him as if the trees and flowers had all turned drab. A terror gnawed at his heart, and he hurried on, more for the need of

movement than with any definite object. And just beyond a
bed of geraniums that had hidden his view she was seated on a
chair, and stopping with a jerk absolutely in front of her, he
said, quite angrily:

'Oh! there you are!'

Which was not a bit the speech with which he had intended
to introduce himself, but served his purpose just as well –
perhaps better.

She did not resent his words or the tone.

'It was the children,' she explained. 'They wanted to play; so
I thought I would come on a little farther.'

Upon which, as a matter of course, he took the chair beside
her, and it did not occur to either of them that they had not
known one another since the beginning, when between
St John's Wood and Albany Street God planted a garden.

(Malvina of Brittany.)

THE DWELLERS IN THE ELMS

It was only a piece of broken glass. From its shape and colour, I should say it had, in its happier days, formed portion of a cheap scent-bottle. Lying isolated on the grass, shone upon by the early morning sun, it certainly appeared at its best. It attracted him.

He cocked his head, and looked at it with his right eye. Then he hopped round to the other side, and looked at it with his left eye. With either optic it seemed equally desirable.

That he was an inexperienced young rook goes without saying. An older bird would not have given a second glance to the thing. Indeed, one would have thought his own instinct might have told him that broken glass would be a mistake in a bird's nest.

But its glitter drew him too strongly for resistance. I am inclined to suspect that at some time, during the growth of his family tree, there must have occurred a *mésalliance,* perhaps worse. Possibly a strain of magpie blood? – one knows the character of magpies, or rather their lack of character – and such things have happened. But I will not pursue further so painful a train: I throw out the suggestion as a possible explanation, that is all.

He hopped nearer. Was it a sweet illusion, this flashing fragment of rainbow; a beautiful vision to fade upon approach, typical of so much that is un-understandable in rook life? He made a dart forward and tapped it with his beak. No, it was real, – as fine a lump of jagged green glass as any newly-married rook could desire, and to be had for the taking. *She* would be pleased with it. He was a well-meaning bird; the mere upward inclination of his tail suggested earnest though possibly ill-directed endeavour.

He turned it over. It was an awkward thing to carry; it had so very many corners. But he succeeded at last in getting it firmly between his beak, and in haste, lest some other bird should seek to dispute with him its possession, at once flew off with it.

A second rook, who had been watching the proceedings from the lime-tree, called to a third who was passing. Even with my limited knowledge of the language I found it easy to follow the conversation; it was so obvious.

'Issachar!'

'Hallo!'

'What do you think? Zebulun's found a piece of broken bottle. He's going to line his nest with it.'

'No!'

'God's truth. Look at him. There he goes; he's got it in his beak.'

'Well, I'm——!'

And they both burst into a laugh.

But Zebulun heeded them not. If he overheard, he probably put down the whole dialogue to jealousy. He made straight for his tree. By standing with my left cheek pressed close against the window-pane, I was able to follow him. He is building in what we call the Paddock elms, – a suburb commenced only last season, but rapidly growing. I wanted to see what his wife would say.

At first she said nothing. He laid it carefully down on the branch near the half-finished nest, and she stretched up her head and looked at it.

Then she looked at him. For about a minute neither spoke. I could see that the situation was becoming strained.

When she did open her beak, it was with a subdued tone, that had a vein of weariness running through it.

'What is it?' she asked.

He was evidently chilled by her manner. As I have explained, he is an inexperienced young rook. This is clearly his first wife, and he stands somewhat in awe of her.

'Well, I don't exactly know what it's *called*,' he answered.

'Oh!'

'No. But it's pretty, isn't it?' he added. He moved it, trying to get it where the sun might reach it. It was evident he was admitting to himself that, seen in the shade, it lost much of its charm.

'Oh, yes; very pretty,' was the rejoinder; 'perhaps you'll tell me what you're going to do with it.'

The question further discomforted him. It was growing upon him that this thing was not going to be the success he had anticipated. It would be necessary to proceed warily.

'Of course it's not a twig,' he began.

'I see it isn't.'

'No. You see, the nest is nearly all twigs as it is, and I thought——'

'Oh, you did think.'

'Yes, my dear. I thought – unless you are of opinion that it's too showy – I thought we might work it in somewhere.'

Then she flared out.

'Oh, did you? You thought that a good idea. An A1 prize idiot I seem to have married, I do. You've been gone twenty minutes, and you bring me back an eight-cornered piece of broken glass, which you think we might "work into" the nest. You'd like to see me sitting on it for a month, you would. You think it would make a nice bed for the children to lie on. You don't think you could manage to find a packet of mixed pins if you went down again, I suppose? They'd look pretty "worked in" somewhere, don't you think? Here, get out of my way. I'll finish this nest by myself.' She always had been short with him.

She caught up the offending object – it was a fairly heavy lump of glass – and flung it out of the tree with all her force. I heard it crash through the cucumber frame. That makes the seventh pane of glass broken in that cucumber frame this week. The couple in the branch above are the worst. Their plan of building is the most extravagant, the most absurd, I ever heard of. They hoist up ten times as much material as they can possibly use; you might think they were going to build a block and let it out in flats to the other rooks. Then what they don't want they fling down again. Suppose we built on such a principle. Suppose a human husband and wife were to start erecting their house in Piccadilly Circus, let us say; and suppose the man spent all the day steadily carrying bricks up the ladder while his wife laid them, never asking her how many she wanted, whether she didn't think he had brought up sufficient, but just accumulating bricks in a senseless fashion, bringing up every brick he could find. And then suppose, when evening came, and looking round they found they had some twenty cartloads of bricks lying unused upon the scaffold, they were to begin flinging them down into Waterloo Place. They would get themselves into trouble; somebody would be sure to speak to them about it. Yet that is precisely what those birds do, and nobody says a word to them. They are supposed to have a President. He lives by himself in the yew-tree outside the morning-room window.

What I want to know is what he is supposed to be good for. This is the sort of thing I want him to look into. I would like him to be worming underneath one evening when those two birds are tidying up; perhaps he would do something then. I have done all I can. I have thrown stones at them that, in the course of nature, have returned to earth again, breaking more glass. I have blazed at them with a revolver; but they have come to regard this proceeding as a mere expression of light-heartedness on my part, possibly confusing me with the Arab of the Desert, who, I am given to understand, expresses himself thus in moments of deep emotion. They merely retire to a safe distance to watch me, no doubt regarding me as a poor performer, inasmuch as I do not also dance and shout between each shot. I have no objection to their building there, if they would only build sensibly. I want somebody to speak to them to whom they will pay attention.

You can hear them in the evening, discussing the matter of this surplus stock.

'Don't you work any more,' he says, as he comes up with the last load; 'you'll tire yourself.'

'Well, I am feeling a bit done up,' she answers, as she hops out of the nest and straightens her back.

'You're a bit peckish, too, I expect,' he adds sympathetically. 'I know I am. We will have a scratch down, and be off.'

'What about all this stuff?' she asks, while titivating herself; 'we'd better not leave it about, it looks so untidy.'

'Oh, we'll soon get rid of that,' he answers. 'I'll have that down in a jiffy.'

To help him, she seizes a stick and is about to drop it. He darts forward and snatches it from her.

'Don't waste that one,' he cries; 'that's a rare one, that is. You see me hit the old man with it.'

And he does. What the gardener says, I will leave you to imagine.

Judged from its structure, the rook family is supposed to come next in intelligence to man himself. Judging from the intelligence displayed by certain human families with whom I have come in contact, I can quite believe it. That rooks talk I am positive. No one can spend half-an-hour watching a rookery without being convinced of this. Whether the talk be always wise and witty, I am not prepared to maintain; but that there is a good deal of it is certain. A young French gentleman of my acquaintance, who visited England to study the language, told me that the impression made upon him by his first social evening in London was that of a parrot-house. Later on, when he came to comprehend, he, of course, recognized the brilliancy and depth of the average London drawing-room talk; but that is how, not comprehending, it impressed him at first. Listening to the riot of a rookery is much the same experience. The conversation to us sounds meaningless; the rooks themselves would probably describe it as sparkling.

(Second Thoughts of an Idle Fellow.)

ON THE ART OF MAKING UP ONE'S MIND

'Now, which would you advise, dear? You see, with the red I shan't be able to wear my magenta hat.'

'Well, then, why not have the grey?'

'Yes, yes, I think the grey will be *more useful*.'

'It's a good material.'

'Yes, and it's a *pretty* grey. You know what I mean, dear; not a *common* grey. Of course grey is always an *uninteresting* colour.'

'It's quiet.'

'And then again, what I feel about the red is that it is so warm-looking. Red makes you *feel* warm even when you're *not* warm. You know what I mean, dear.'

'Well, then, why not have the red? It suits you – red.'

'No; do you really think so?'

'Well, when you've got a colour, I mean, of course.'

'Yes, that *is* the drawback to red. No, I think, on the whole, the grey is *safer*.'

'Then you will take the grey, madam.'

'Yes, I think I'd better; don't you, dear?'

'I like it myself very much.'

'And it is good wearing stuff. I shall have it trimmed with—— Oh! you haven't cut it off, have you?'

'I was just about to, madam.'

'Well, don't for a moment. Just let me have another look at the red. You see, dear, it has just occurred to me – that chinchilla would look so well on the red.'

'So it would, dear.'

'And, you see, I've *got* the chinchilla.'

'Then have the red. Why not?'

'Well, there is the hat I'm thinking of.'

'You haven't anything else you could wear with that?'

'Nothing at all, and it would go so *beautifully* with the grey. Yes, I think I'll have the grey. It's always a safe colour, – grey.'

'Fourteen yards I think you said, madam?'

'Yes, fourteen yards will be enough; because I shall mix it with – one minute. You see, dear, if I take the grey I shall have nothing to wear with my black jacket.'

'Won't it go with grey?'

'Not well – not so well as with red.'

'I should have the red, then. You evidently fancy it yourself.'

'No, personally I prefer the grey. But then one must think of *everything,* and—— Good gracious! that's surely not the right time?'

'No, madam, it's ten minutes slow. We always keep our clocks a little slow.'

'And we were to have been at Madame Jannaway's at a quarter past twelve. How long shopping does take! Why, whatever time did we start?'

'About eleven, wasn't it?'

'Half-past ten. I remember now; because, you know, we said we'd start at half-past nine. We've been two hours already!'

'And we don't seem to have done much, do we?'

'Done literally nothing, and I meant to have done *so* much. I *must* go to Madame Jannaway's. Have you got my purse, dear? Oh, it's all right, I've got it.'

'Well, *now* you haven't decided whether you're going to have the grey or the red.'

'I'm sure I don't know what I *do* want now. I had made up my mind a minute ago, and now it's all gone again – oh, yes, I remember, the red. Yes, I'll have the red. No, I don't mean the red; I mean the grey.'

140

'Now, which would you advise, dear?'

'You were talking about the red last time, if you remember, dear.'

'Oh, so I was; you're quite right. That's the worst of shopping. Do you know, I get quite confused sometimes.'

'Then you will decide on the red, madam?'

'Yes, yes, I shan't do any better, shall I, dear? What do *you* think? You haven't got any other shades of red, have you? This is such an *ugly* red.'

The shopman reminds her that she has seen all the other reds, and that this is the particular shade she selected and admired.

'Oh, very well, she replies, with the air of one from whom all earthly cares are falling, 'I must take that, then, I suppose. I can't be worried about it any longer. I've wasted half the morning already.'

Outside she recollects three insuperable objections to the red, and four unanswerable arguments why she should have selected the grey. She wonders would they change it, if she went back and asked to see the shop-walker? Her friend, who wants her lunch, thinks not.

'That is what I hate about shopping,' she says. 'One never has time to really *think*.'

(Second Thoughts of an Idle Fellow.)

ON THE INADVISABILITY OF FOLLOWING ADVICE

'There are people like that,' he broke out, as we turned, 'people who will go about giving advice. I'll be getting six months over one of them, I'm always afraid. I remember a pony I had once.' (I judged the man to be a small farmer; he talked in a wurzelly tone. I don't know if you understand what I mean, but an atmosphere of wurzels was the thing that somehow he suggested.) 'It was a thorough-bred Welsh pony, as sound a little beast as ever stepped. I'd had him out to grass all the winter, and one day in the early spring I thought I'd take him for a run. I had to go to Amersham on business. I put him into the cart, and drove him across; it is just ten miles from my place. He was a bit uppish, and had lathered himself pretty freely by the time we reached the town.

'A man was at the door of the hotel. He says, "That's a good pony of yours."

'"Pretty middling," I says.

'"It doesn't do to overdrive 'em when they're young," he says.

'I says, "He's done ten miles, and I've done most of the pulling. I reckon I'm a jolly sight more exhausted than he is."

'I went inside and did my business, and when I came out the man was still there. "Going back up the hill?" he says to me.

'Somehow I didn't cotton to him from the beginning. "Well, I've got to get the other side of it," I says; "and unless you know any patent way of getting over a hill without going up it, I reckon I am."

'He says, "You take my advice: give him a pint of old ale before you start."

"'Old ale," I says; "why, he's a teetotaler."

"'Never you mind that," he answers; "you give him a pint of old ale. I know these ponies; he's a good 'un, but he ain't set. A pint of old ale, and he'll take you up that hill like a cable tramway, and not hurt himself.'"

'I don't know what it is about this class of man. One asks oneself afterwards why one didn't knock his hat over his eyes and run his head into the nearest horse-trough. But at the time one listens to them. I got a pint of old ale in a hand bowl, and brought it out. About half-a-dozen chaps were standing round, and of course there was a good deal of chaff.

"'You're starting him on the downward course, Jim," says one of them. "He'll take to gambling, rob a bank, and murder his mother. That's always the result of a glass of ale, 'cording to the tracts."

"'He won't drink it like that," says another; "it's as flat as ditch water. Put a head on it for him."

"'Ain't you got a cigar for him?" says a third.

"'A cup of coffee and a round of buttered toast would do him a sight more good, a cold day like this," says a fourth.

'I'd half a mind then to throw the stuff away, or drink it myself; it seemed a piece of bally nonsense, giving good ale to a four-year-old pony; but the moment the beggar smelt the bowl he reached out his head, and lapped it up as though he'd been a Christian; and I jumped into the cart and started off, amid cheers. We got up the hill pretty steady. Then the liquor began to work into his head. I've taken home a drunken man more than once; and there's pleasanter jobs than that. I've seen a drunken woman, and they're worse. But a drunken Welsh pony I never want to have anything more to do with so long as I live. Having four legs, he managed to hold himself up; but as to guiding himself, he couldn't; and as for letting me do it, he wouldn't. First we were one side of the road, and then we were the other. When we were not either side, we were crossways in the middle. I heard a bicycle bell behind me, but I dared not turn my head. All I could do was to shout to the fellow to keep where he was.

'"I want to pass you," he sang out, so soon as he was near enough.

'"Well, you can't do it," I called back.

'"Why can't I?" he answered. "How much of the road do *you* want?"

'"All of it, and a bit over," I answered him, "for this job, and nothing in the way."

'He followed me for half a mile, abusing me; and every time he thought he saw a chance he tried to pass me. But the pony was always a bit too smart for him. You might have thought the brute was doing it on purpose.

'"You're not fit to be driving." he shouted. He was quite right; I wasn't. I was feeling just about dead beat.

'"What do you think you are," he continued, – "a musical ride?" (He was a common sort of fellow.) "Who sent *you* home with the washing?"

'Well, he was making me wild by this time. "What's the good of talking to me?" I shouted back. "Come and blackguard the pony if you want to blackguard anybody. I've got all I can do without the help of that alarm clock of yours. Go away; you're only making him worse."

'"What's the matter with the pony?" he called out.

'"Can't you see?" I answered. "He's drunk."

'Well, of course it sounded foolish; the truth often does.

'"One of you's drunk," he retorted; "for two pins I'd come and haul you out of the cart."

'I wish to goodness he had! I'd have given something to be out of that cart. But he didn't have the chance. At that moment the pony gave a sudden swerve; and I take it he must have been a bit too close. I heard a yell and a curse, and at the same instant I was splashed from head to foot with ditch-water. Then the brute bolted. A man was coming along, asleep on the top of a cartload of Windsor chairs. It's disgraceful the way those wagoners go to sleep; I wonder there are not more accidents. I don't think he ever knew what had happened to him. I couldn't look round to see what became of him; I only saw him start. Halfway down the hill a policeman holla'd to me to stop; I heard him shouting out something about furious driving. Half a mile this side of Chesham we came upon a girls' school walking two and two – a "crocodile," they call it, I think. I bet you those girls are still talking about it. It must have taken the old woman a good hour to collect them together again.

'It was market day in Chesham; and I guess there has not been a busier market-day in Chesham before or since. We went through the town at about thirty miles an hour. I've never seen Chesham so lively, it's a sleepy hole as a rule. A mile outside the town I sighted the High Wycombe coach. I didn't feel I minded much; I had got to that pass when it didn't seem to matter to me what happened; I only felt curious. A dozen yards off the coach the pony stopped dead; that jerked me off the seat to the bottom of the cart. I couldn't get up because the seat was on top of me. I could see nothing but the sky, and occasionally the head of the pony, when he stood upon his hind legs. But I could hear what the driver of the coach said, and I judged he was having trouble also.

'"Take that damn circus out of the road," he shouted. If he'd had any sense, he'd have seen how helpless I was. I could hear his cattle plunging about; they are like that, horses, – if they see one fool, then they all want to be fools.

'"Take it home, and tie it up to its organ," shouted the guard.

'Then an old woman went into hysterics, and began laughing like a hyena. That started the pony off again, and, as far as I could calculate by watching the clouds, we did another four miles at the gallop. Then he thought he'd try to jump a gate, and finding, I suppose, that the cart hampered him, he started kicking it to pieces. I'd never have thought a cart could have been separated into so many pieces, if I hadn't seen it done. When he had got rid of everything but half a wheel and the splashboard he bolted again. I remained behind with the other ruins, and glad I was to get a little rest. He came back later in the afternoon, and I was pleased to sell him the next week for a five-pound note: it cost me about another ten to repair myself.

'To this day, I am chaffed about that pony, and the local Temperance Society made a lecture out of me. That's what comes of following advice.'

(Second Thoughts of an Idle Fellow.)

THE ANGEL AND THE AUTHOR

I had a vexing dream one night, not long ago: it was about a fortnight after Christmas. I dreamt I flew out of the window in my nightshirt. I went up and up. I was glad that I was going up. 'They have been noticing me,' I thought to myself. 'If anything, I have been a bit too good. A little less virtue and I might have lived longer. But one cannot have everything.' The world grew smaller and smaller. The last I saw of London was the long line of electric lamps bordering the Embankment; later nothing remained but a faint luminosity buried beneath darkness. It was at this point of my journey that I heard behind me the slow, throbbing sound of wings.

I turned my head. It was the Recording Angel. He had a weary look; I judged him to be tired.

'Yes,' he acknowledged, 'it is a trying period for me, your Christmas time.'

'I am sure it must be,' I returned; 'the wonder to me is how you get through it all. You see at Christmas time,' I went on, 'all we men and women become generous, quite suddenly. It is really a delightful sensation.'

'You are to be envied,' he agreed.

'It is the first Christmas number that starts me off,' I told him; 'those beautiful pictures – the sweet child looking so pretty in her furs, giving Bovril with her own dear little hands to the shivering street arab; the good old red-faced squire shovelling out plum pudding to the crowd of grateful villagers. It makes me yearn to borrow a collecting box and go round doing good myself.

'And it is not only me – I should say I,' I continued; 'I don't want you to run away with the idea that I am the only good man in the world. That's what I like about Christmas, it makes everybody good. The lovely sentiments we go about repeating! the noble deeds we do! from a little while before Christmas up to, say, the end of January! why noting them down must be a comfort to you.'

'Yes,' he admitted, 'noble deeds are always a great joy to me.'

'They are to all of us,' I say; 'I love to think of all the good deeds I myself have done. I have often thought of keeping a diary – jotting them down each day. It would be so nice for one's children.'

He agreed there was an idea in this.

'That book of yours,' I said, 'I suppose, now, it contains all the good actions that we men and women have been doing during the last six weeks?' It was a bulky looking volume.

Yes, he answered, they were all recorded in the book.

It was more for the sake of talking than anything else that I kept up with him. I did not really doubt his care and conscientiousness, but it is always pleasant to chat about one's self. 'My five shillings subscription to the *Daily Telegraph's* Sixpenny fund for the Unemployed – got that down all right?' I asked him.

Yes, he replied, it was entered.

'As a matter of fact, now I come to think of it, I added, 'it was ten shillings altogether. They spelt my name wrong the first time.'

Both subscriptions had been entered, he told me.

'Then I have been to four charity dinners,' I reminded him; 'I forget what the particular charity was about. I know I suffered the next morning. Champagne never does agree with me. But, then, if you don't order it people think you can't afford it, Not that I don't like it. It's my liver, if you understand. If I take more——'

He interrupted me with the assurance that my attendance had been noted.

'Last week I sent a dozen photographs of myself, signed, to a charity bazaar.'

He said he remembered my doing so.

'Then let me see,' I continued, 'I have been to two ordinary balls. I don't care much about dancing, but a few of us generally play a little bridge; and to one fancy dress affair. I went as Sir Walter Raleigh. Some men cannot afford to show their leg. What I say is, if a man can, why not? It isn't often that one gets the opportunity of really looking one's best.'

He told me all three balls had been duly entered; and commented upon.

'And, of course, you remember my performance of Talbot Champneys in *Our Boys* the week before last, in aid of the Fund of Poor Curates,' I went on. 'I don't know whether you saw the notice in the *Morning Post*, but——'

He again interrupted me to remark that what the *Morning Post* man said would be entered, one way or the other, to the critic of the *Morning Post*, and had nothing to do with me. 'Of course not,' I agreed; 'and between ourselves, I don't think the charity got very much. Expenses, when you come to add refreshments and one thing and another, mount up. But I fancy they rather liked my Talbot Champneys.'

He replied that he had been present at the performance, and had made his own report.

I also reminded him of the four balcony seats I had taken for the monster show at His Majesty's in aid of the Fund for the Destitute British in Johannesburg. Not all the celebrated actors and actresses announced on the posters had appeared, but all had sent letters full of kindly wishes; and the others – all the celebrities one had never heard of – had turned up to a man. Still, on the whole, the show was well worth the money. There was nothing to grumble at.

There were other noble deeds of mine. I could not remember them at the time in their entirety. I seemed to have done a good many. But I did remember the rummage sale to which I sent all my old clothes, including a coat that had got mixed up with them by accident, and that I believe I could have worn again. And also the raffle I had joined for a motor-car.

The Angel said I really need not be alarmed, that everything had been noted, together with other matters I, may be, had forgotten.

I felt a certain curiosity. We had been getting on very well together – at least, so it had seemed to me. I asked him if he would mind my seeing the book. He said there could be no objection. He opened it at the page devoted to myself, and I flew a little higher, and looked down over his shoulder. I can hardly believe it, even now – that I could have dreamt anything so foolish:

He had got it all down wrong!

Instead of to the credit side of my account he had put the whole bag of tricks to my debit. He had mixed them up with my sins – with acts of hypocrisy, vanity, self-indulgence. Under the head of Charity he had but one item to my credit for the past six months: my giving up my seat inside a tramcar late one wet night, to a dismal-looking old woman, who had not even the politeness to say 'thank you', she seemed just half asleep. According to this idiot, all the time and money I had spent responding to these charitable appeals had been wasted.

I was not angry with him, at first. I was willing to regard what he had done as merely a clerical error.

'You have got the items down all right,' I said (I spoke quite friendly), 'but you have made a slight mistake – we all do now and again: you have put them down on the wrong side of the book. I only hope this sort of thing doesn't occur often.'

What irritated me as much as anything was the grave, passionless face the Angel turned upon me.

'There is no mistake,' he answered.

'No mistake!' I cried. 'Why, you blundering——'

He closed the book with a weary sigh.

I felt so mad with him, I went to snatch it out of his hand.

He did not do anything that I was aware of, but at once I began falling. The faint luminosity beneath me grew, and then the lights of London seemed shooting up to meet me. I was coming down on the clock tower at Westminster. I gave myself a convulsive twist, hoping to escape it, and fell into the river.

And then I awoke.

But it stays with me: the weary sadness of the Angel's face.

(The Angel and the Author.)

HOW TO BE HEALTHY AND UNHAPPY

'There was a gent in Middle Temple Lane,' said Mrs Wilkins, 'as I used to do for. It's my belief as 'e killed 'imself worrying twenty-four hours a day over what 'e called 'is 'ygiene.

'Leastways 'e's dead and buried now, which must be a comfort to 'imself, feeling as at last 'e's out of danger. All 'is time 'e spent taking care of 'imself – didn't seem to 'ave a leisure moment in which to live. For 'alf an hour every morning 'e'd lie on 'is back on the floor, which is a draughty place, I always 'old, at the best of times, with nothing on but 'is pyjamas, waving 'is arms and legs about, and twisting 'imself into shapes unnatural to a Christian. Then 'e found out that everything 'e'd been doing on 'is back was just all wrong, so 'e turned over and did tricks on 'is stomach – begging your pardon for using the word – that you'd 'ave thought more fit and proper to a worm than to a man. Then all that was discovered to be a mistake. There don't seem nothing certain in these matters. That's the awkward part of it, so it seems to me. 'E got 'imself a machine, by means of which 'e'd 'ang 'imself up to the wall, and behave for all the world like a beetle with a pin stuck through 'im, poor thing. It used to give me the shudders to catch sight of 'im through the 'alf-open door. For that was part of the game: you 'ad to 'ave a current of air through the room, the result of which was that for six months out of the year 'e'd

be coughing and blowing 'is nose from morning to night. It
was the new treatment, so 'e'd explain to me. You got yourself
accustomed to draughts so that they didn't 'urt you, and if you
died in the process that only proved that you never ought to
'ave been born.

'Then there came in this new Japanese business, and 'e'd 'ire a little
smiling 'eathen to chuck 'im
about 'is room for 'alf an hour
every morning after breakfast. It got on my nerves
after a while 'earing 'im
being bumped on the
floor every minute, or flung
with 'is 'ead into the fire-place.
But 'e always said it was doing 'im
good. 'E'd argue that it freshened up
'is liver. It was 'is liver that 'e seemed to
live for – didn't appear to 'ave any other
interest in life. It was the same with 'is
food. One year it would be nothing
but meat, and next door to raw at
that. One of them medical papers, 'ad suddenly discovered that
we were intended to be a sort of wild beast. The wonder to me
is that 'e didn't go out 'unting chickens with a club, and bring
'em 'ome and eat 'em on the mat without any further fuss. For
drink it would be boiling water that burnt my fingers merely
'andling the glass. Then some other crank came out with the
information that every other crank was wrong – which, taken
by itself, sounds natural enough – that meat was fatal to the
'uman system. Upon that 'e becomes all at once a raging,
tearing vegetarian, and trouble enough I 'ad learning twenty
different ways of cooking beans, which didn't make, so far as I
could ever see, the slightest difference – beans they were, and
beans they tasted like, whether you called them *ragoût à la*

maison, or cutlets *à la Pompadour*. But it seemed to please 'im.

'Then vegetarianism turned out to be the mistake of our lives. It seemed we made an error giving up monkeys' food. That was our natural victuals; nuts with occasional bananas. As I used to tell 'im, if that was so, then for all we 'ad got out of it we might just as well 'ave stopped up a tree – saved rent and shoe leather. But 'e was one of that sort that don't seem able to 'elp believing everything they read in print. If one of those papers 'ad told 'im to live on the shells and throw away the nuts, 'e'd have made a conscientious endeavour to do so, contending that 'is failure to digest them was merely the result of vicious training – didn't seem to 'ave any likes or dislikes of 'is own. You might 'ave thought 'e was just a bit of public property made to be experimented upon.

'One of the daily papers interviewed an old gent, as said 'e was a 'undred, and I will say from 'is picture as any'ow 'e looked it. 'E said it was all the result of never 'aving swallowed anything 'ot, upon which my gentleman for a week lives on cold porridge, if you'll believe me; although myself I'd rather 'ave died at fifty and got it over. Then another paper dug up from somewhere a sort of animated corpse that said 'e was a 'undred and two, and attributed the unfortunate fact to 'is always 'aving 'ad 'is food as 'ot as 'e could swallow it. A bit of sense did begin to dawn upon 'im then, but too late in the day, I take it. 'E'd played about with 'imself too long. 'E died at thirty-two, looking to all appearance sixty, and you can't say as 'ow it was the result of not taking advice.

'We talk a lot about it,' thought Mrs Wilkins, 'but it does not seem to me that we are very much better off than before we took to worrying ourselves for twenty-four 'ours a day about 'ow we are going to live. Lord! to read the advertisements in the papers you would think as 'ow flesh and blood was never intended to 'ave any natural ills. "Do you ever 'ave a pain in your back?" because, if so, there's a picture of a kind gent who's willing for one and sixpence halfpenny to take it quite away from you – make you look forward to scrubbing floors, and standing over the wash-tub six hours at a stretch like to a beanfeast. "Do you ever feel as though you don't want to get out of bed in the morning?" that's all to be cured by a bottle of their stuff – or two at the outside. Four children to keep, and a sick 'usband on your 'ands used to get me over it when I was younger. I used to fancy it was just because I was tired.

'There's some of them seem to think,' continued Mrs Wilkins, 'that if you don't get all you want out of this world, and ain't so 'appy as you've persuaded yourself you ought to be, that it's all because you ain't taking the right medicine. Appears to me there's only one doctor as can do for you, all the others talk as though they could, and 'e only comes to each of us once, and then 'e makes no charge.'

(The Angel and the Author.)

SWALLOW STREET

Every summer I suffer much from indignation. I love to watch
the swallows building. They build beneath the eaves outside
my study window. Such cheerful little chatter-boxes they are.
Long after sunset, when all the other birds are sleeping, the
swallows still are chattering softly. It sounds as if they were
telling one another some pretty story, and often I am sure there
must be humour in it, for every now and then one hears a little
twittering laugh. I delight in having them there, so close to me.
The fancy comes to me that one day, when my brain has grown
more cunning, I, too, listening in the twilight, shall hear the
stories that they tell.

One or two phrases already I have come to understand:
'Once upon a time' – 'Long, long ago' – 'In a strange, far-off
land.' I hear these words so constantly, I am sure I have them
right. I call it 'Swallow Street,' this row of six or seven nests.
Two or three, like villas in their own grounds, stand alone, and
others are semi-detached. It makes me angry that the sparrows
will come and steal them. The sparrows will hang about
deliberately waiting for a pair of swallows to finish their nest,
and then, with a brutal laugh that makes my blood boil, drive
the swallows away and take possession of it. And the swallows
are so wonderfully patient.

'Never mind, old girl,' says Tommy Swallow, after the first
big cry is over, to Jenny Swallow, 'let's try again.'

And half an hour later, full of fresh plans, they are choosing
another likely site, chattering cheerfully once more. I watched
the building of a particular nest for nearly a fortnight one year;
and when, after two or three days' absence, I returned and

found a pair of sparrows comfortably ensconced therein, I just felt mad. I saw Mrs Sparrow looking out. Maybe my anger was working upon my imagination, but it seemed to me that she nodded to me:

'Nice little house, ain't it? What I call well built.'

Mr Sparrow then flew up with a gaudy feather, dyed blue, which belonged to me. I recognized it. It had come out of the brush with which the girl breaks the china ornaments in our drawing-room. At any other time I should have been glad to see him flying off with the whole thing, handle included. But now I felt the theft of that one feather as an added injury. Mrs Sparrow chirped with delight at sight of the gaudy monstrosity. Having got the house cheap, they were going to spend their small amount of energy upon internal decoration. That was their idea clearly, a 'Liberty interior.' She looked more like a Cockney sparrow than a country one – had been born and bred in Regent Street, no doubt.

'There's not much justice in this world,' said I to myself; 'but there's going to be some introduced into this business – that is, if I can find a ladder.'

I did find a ladder, and fortunately it was long enough.

Mr and Mrs Sparrow were out when I arrived, possibly on the hunt for cheap photo frames and Japanese fans. I did not want to make a mess. I removed the house neatly into a dust-pan, and wiped the street clear of every trace of it. I had just put back the ladder when Mrs Sparrow returned with a piece of pink cotton-wool in her mouth. That was her idea of a colour scheme: apple-blossom pink and Reckett's blue side by side. She dropped her wool and sat on the water-spout, and tried to understand things.

'Number one, number two, number four; where the blazes' – sparrows are essentially common, and the women are as bad as the men – 'is number three?'

Mr Sparrow came up from behind, over the roof. He was carrying a piece of yellow-fluff, part of a lampshade, as far as I could judge.

'Move yourself,' he said, 'what's the sense of sitting there in the rain?'

'I went out just for a moment,' replied Mrs Sparrow; 'I could not have been gone, no, not a couple of minutes. When I came back——'

'Oh, get indoors,' said Mr Sparrow, 'talk about it there.'

'It's what I'm telling you,' continued Mrs Sparrow, 'if you would only listen. There isn't any door, there isn't any house——'

'Isn't any——' Mr Sparrow, holding on to the rim of the spout, turned himself topsy-turvy and surveyed the street. From where I was standing behind the laurel bushes I could see nothing but his back. He stood up again, looking angry and flushed.

'What have you done with the house? Can't I turn my back a minute——'

'I ain't done nothing with it. As I keep on telling you, I had only just gone——'

'Oh, bother where you had gone. Where's the darned house gone? That's what I want to know.'

They looked at one another. If ever astonishment was expressed in the attitude of a bird it was told by the tails of those two sparrows. They whispered wickedly together. The idea occurred to them that by force or cunning they might perhaps obtain possession of one of the other nests. But all the other nests were occupied, and even gentle Jenny Swallow, once in her own home with the children round about her, is not to be trifled with. Mr Sparrow called at number two, put his head in at the door, and then returned to the waterspout.

'Lady says we don't live there,' he explained to Mrs Sparrow. There was silence for a while.

'Not what I call a classy street,' commented Mrs Sparrow.

'If it were not for that terrible tired feeling of mine,' said Mr Sparrow, 'blame if I wouldn't build a house of my own.'

'Perhaps,' said Mrs Sparrow, – 'I have heard it said that a

little bit of work, now and then, does you good.'

'All sorts of wild ideas about in the air nowadays,' said Mr Sparrow, 'it don't do to listen to everybody.'

'And it don't do to sit still and do nothing neither,' snapped Mrs Sparrow. 'I don't want to have to forget I'm a lady, but – well, any man who was a man would see things for himself.'

'Why did I ever marry?' retorted Mr Sparrow.

They flew away together, quarrelling.

(Idle Ideas in 1905.)

SHOULD WE SAY WHAT WE THINK?

A mad friend of mine will have it that the characteristic of the age is Make-Believe. He argues that all social intercourse is founded on make-believe. A servant enters to say that Mr and Mrs Bore are in the drawing-room.

'Oh, damn!' says the man.

'Hush!' says the woman. 'Shut the door, Susan. How often am I to tell you never to leave the door open?'

The man creeps upstairs on tiptoe and shuts himself in his study. The woman does things before a looking-glass, waits till she feels she is sufficiently mistress of herself not to show her feelings, and then enters the drawing-room with outstretched hands and the look of one welcoming an angel's visit. She says how delighted she is to see the Bores – how good it was of them to

Mr and Mrs Bore are in the drawing-room.

come. Why did they not bring more Bores with them? Where is naughty Bore junior? Why does he never come to see her now? She will have to be really angry with him. And sweet little Flossie Bore? Too young to pay calls! Nonsense. An 'At Home' day is not worth having where all the Bores are not.

The Bores, who had hoped that she was out – who have only called because the etiquette book told them that they must call at least four times in the season, explain how they have been trying and trying to come.

'This afternoon,' recounts Mrs Bore, 'we were determined to come. "John, dear," I said this morning, "I shall go and see dear Mrs Bounder this afternoon, no matter what happens."'

The idea conveyed is that the Prince of Wales, on calling at the Bores, was told that he could not come in. He might call again in the evening or come some other day. That afternoon the Bores were going to enjoy themselves in their own way; they were going to see Mrs Bounder.

'And how is Mr Bounder?' demands Mrs Bore.

Mrs Bounder remains mute for a moment, straining her ears. She can hear him creeping past the door on his way downstairs. She hears the front door softly opened and closed-to. She wakes, as from a dream. She has been thinking of the sorrow that will fall on Bounder when he returns home later and learns what he has missed.

And thus it is, not only with the Bores and Bounders, but even with us who are not Bores or Bounders. Society in all ranks is founded on the make-believe that everybody is charming; that we are delighted to see everybody; that everybody is delighted to see us; that it is so good of everybody to come; that we are desolate at the thought that they really must go now.

Which would we rather do – stop and finish our cigar or hasten into the drawing-room to hear Miss Screecher sing? Can you ask us? We tumble over each other in our hurry. Miss

Screecher would really rather not sing; but if we insist—— We do insist. Miss Screecher, with pretty reluctance, consents. We are careful not to look at one another. We sit with our eyes fixed on the ceiling. Miss Screecher finishes, and rises.

'But it was so short,' we say, so soon as we can be heard above the applause. Is Miss Screecher quite sure that was the whole of it? Or has she been playing tricks upon us, the naughty lady, defrauding us of a verse? Miss Screecher assures us that the fault is the composer's. But she knows another. At this hint, our faces lighten again with gladness. We clamour for more.

Our host's wine is always the most extraordinary we have tasted. No, not another glass; we dare not – doctor's orders, very strict. Our host's cigars! We did not know they made such cigars in this workaday world. No, we really could not smoke another. Well, if he will be so pressing, may we put it in our pocket? The truth is, we are not used to high smoking. Our hostess's coffee! Would she confide to us her secret? The baby! We hardly trust ourselves to speak. The usual baby – we have seen it. As a rule, to be candid, we never could detect much beauty in babies – have always held the usual gush about them to be insincere. But this baby! We are almost on the point of asking them where they got it. It is just the kind we wanted for ourselves. Little Janet's recitation: 'A Visit to the Dentist!' Hitherto the amateur reciter has not appealed to us. But this is genius, surely. She ought to be trained for the stage. Her mother does not altogether approve of the stage. We plead for the stage – that it may not be deprived of such talent.

Every bride is beautiful. Every bride looks charming in a simple costume of – for further particulars see local papers. Every marriage is a cause for universal rejoicing. With our wine-glass in our hand we picture the ideal life we know to be in store for them. How can it be otherwise? She, the daughter of her mother. (Cheers.) He – well, we all know him. (More cheers.) Also involuntary guffaw from ill-regulated young man at end of table, promptly suppressed.

We carry our make-believe even into our religion. We sit in church, and in voices swelling with pride, mention to the Almighty, at stated intervals, that we are miserable worms – that there is no good in us. This sort of thing, we gather, is expected of us; it does us no harm, and is supposed to please.

(Idle Ideas in 1905.)

WHY DIDN'T HE MARRY THE GIRL?

What is wrong with marriage, anyhow? I find myself pondering this question so often, when reading high-class literature. I put it to myself again the other evening, during a performance of *Faust*. Why could not Faust have married the girl? I would not have married her myself for any consideration whatsoever; but that is not the argument. Faust, apparently, could not see anything amiss with her. Both of them were mad about each other. Yet the idea of a quiet, unostentatious marriage with a week's honeymoon, say, in Vienna, followed by a neat little cottage *orné,* not too far from Nürnberg, so that their friends could have come out to them, never seems to have occurred to either of them.

There could have been a garden. Marguerite might have kept chickens and a cow. That sort of girl, brought up to hard work and by no means too well educated, is all the better for having something to do. Later, with the gradual arrival of the family, a good, all-round woman might have been hired in to assist. Faust, of course, would have had his study and got to work again; that would have kept him out of further mischief. The idea that a brainy man, his age, was going to be happy with nothing to do all day but fool round a petticoat was ridiculous from the beginning. Valentine – a good fellow, Valentine, with nice ideas – would have spent his Saturdays to Monday with them. Over a pipe and a glass of wine, he and Faust would have discussed the local politics.

He would have danced the children on his knee, have told them tales about the war – taught the eldest boy to shoot. Faust, with a practical man like Valentine to help him, would probably have invented a new gun. Valentine would have got it taken up. Things might have come of it. Sybil, in course of time, would have married and settled down – perhaps have taken a little house near to them. He and Marguerite would have joked – when Mrs Sybil was not around – about his early infatuation. The old mother would have toddled over from Nürnberg – not too often, just for the day.

The picture grows upon one the more one thinks of it. Why did it never occur to them? There would have been a bit of a bother with the Old Man. I can imagine Mephistopheles being upset about it, thinking himself swindled. Of course, if that was the reason – if Faust said to himself:

'I should like to marry the girl, but I won't do it; it would not be fair to the Old Man; he has been to a lot of trouble working this thing up; in common gratitude I cannot turn round now and behave like a decent sensible man; it would not be playing the game' – if this was the way Faust looked at the matter there is nothing more to be said. Indeed, it shows him in rather a fine light – noble, if quixotic.

If, on the other hand, he looked at the question from the point of view of himself and the girl, I think the thing might have been managed. All one had to do in those days when one wanted to get rid of the Devil was to show him a sword hilt. Faust and Marguerite could have slipped into a church one morning, and have kept him out of the way with a sword hilt till the ceremony was through. They might have hired a small boy:

'You see the gentleman in red? Well, he wants us and we don't want him. That is the only difference between us. Now, you take this sword, and when you see him coming show him the hilt. Don't hurt him; just show him the sword and shake your head. He will understand.'

The old gentleman's expression, when subsequently Faust presented him to Marguerite, would have been interesting:

'Allow me, my wife. My dear, a – a friend of mine. You may

remember meeting him that night at your aunt's.'

As I have said, there would have been ructions; but I do not myself see what could have been done. There was nothing in the bond to the effect that Faust should not marry, so far as we are told. The Old Man had a sense of humour. My own opinion is that, after getting over the first annoyance, he himself would have seen the joke. I can even picture him looking in now and again on Mr and Mrs Faust. The children would be hurried off to bed. There would be, for a while, an atmosphere of constraint.

But the Old Man had a way with him. He would have told one or two stories at which Marguerite would have blushed, at which Faust would have grinned. I can see the old fellow occasionally joining the homely social board. The children, awed at first, would have sat silent with staring eyes. But, as I have said, the Old Man had a way with him. Why should he not have reformed? The good woman's unconsciously exerted influence – the sweet childish prattle! One hears of such things. Might he not have come to be known as 'Nunkie'?

(Idle Ideas in 1905.)

TOO MUCH LOVER

'I knew a girl,' I said, 'or, rather, a young married woman, who was cured of folly by the homoeopathic method. Her great trouble was that her husband had ceased to be her lover.'

'It seems to me so sad,' said the Old Maid. 'Sometimes it is the woman's fault, sometimes the man's; more often both. The little courtesies, the fond words, the tender nothings that mean so much to those that love – it would cost so little not to forget them, and they would make life so much more beautiful.'

'There is a line of common-sense running through all things,' I replied; 'the secret of life consists in not diverging far from it on either side. He had been the most devoted wooer, never happy out of her eyes; but before they had been married a year she found to her astonishment that he could be content even away from her skirts, that he actually took pains to render himself agreeable to other women. He would spend whole afternoons at his club, slip out for a walk occasionally by himself, shut himself up now and again in his study. It went so far that one day he expressed a distinct desire to leave her for a week and go a-fishing with some other men. She never complained – at least, not to him.'

'That is where she was foolish,' said the Girton Girl. 'Silence in such cases is a mistake. The other party does not know what is the matter with you, and you yourself – your temper bottled up within – become more disagreeable every day.'

'She confided her trouble to a friend,' I explained.

'I so dislike people who do that,' said the Woman of the World. 'Emily never would speak to George; she would come and complain about him to me, as if I were responsible for him: I wasn't even his mother. When she had finished, George would come along, and I had to listen to the whole thing over again from his point of view. I got so tired of it at last that I determined to stop it.'

'How did you succeed?' asked the Old Maid, who appeared to be interested in the recipe.

'I knew George was coming one afternoon,' explained the Woman of the World. 'so I persuaded Emily to wait in the conservatory. She thought I was going to give him good advice; instead of that I sympathized with him and encouraged him to speak his mind freely, which he did. It made her so mad that she came out and told him what she thought of him. I left them at it. They were both of them the better for it; and so was I.'

'In my case,' I said, 'it came about differently. Her friend explained to him just what was happening. She pointed out to him how his neglect and indifference were slowly alienating from him his wife's affections. He argued the subject.

'"But a lover and a husband are not the same," he contended; "the situation is entirely different. You run after somebody you want to overtake; but when you have caught him up, you settle down quietly and walk beside him; you don't continue shouting and waving your handkerchief after you have gained him."

'Their mutual friend presented the problem differently.

'"You must hold what you have won," she said, "or it will slip away from you. By a certain course of conduct and behaviour you gained a sweet girl's regard; show yourself other than you were, how can you expect her to think the same of you?"

'"You mean," he inquired, "that I should talk and act as her husband exactly as I did when her lover?"

'"Precisely," said the friend; "why not?"

'"It seems to me a mistake," he grumbled.

'"Try it and see," said the friend.

'"All right," he said, "I will." And he went straight home and set to work.'

'Was it too late,' asked the Old Maid, 'or did they come together again?'

'For the next month,' I answered, 'they were together twenty-four hours of the day. And then it was the wife who suggested, like the poet in Gilbert's "Patience", the delight with which she would welcome an occasional afternoon off.

'He hung about her while she was dressing in the morning. Just as she had got her hair fixed he would kiss it passionately and it would come down again. All meal time he would hold her hand under the table and insist on feeding her with a fork. Before marriage he had behaved once or twice in this sort of way at picnics; and after marriage, when at breakfast-time he had sat at the other end of the table reading the paper or his letters, she had reminded him of it reproachfully. The entire day he never left her side. She could never read a book; instead, he would read to her aloud, generally Browning's poems or translations from Goethe. Reading aloud was not an accomplishment of his, but in their courting days she had expressed herself pleased at his attempts, and of this he took care, in his turn, to remind her. It was his idea that if the game were played at all, she should take a hand also. If he was to blither, it was only fair that she should bleat back. As he explained, for the future they would both be lovers all their life long; and no logical argument in reply could she think of. If she tried to write a letter, he would snatch away the paper her dear hands were pressing and fall to kissing it – and, of course, smearing it. When he wasn't giving her pins and needles by sitting on her feet he was balancing himself on the arm of her chair and occasionally falling over on top of her. If she went shopping, he went with her and made himself ridiculous at the dressmaker's. In society he took no notice of anybody but of her, and was hurt if she spoke to anybody but to him. Not that it was often, during that month, that they did see any society;

most invitations he refused for them both, reminding her how once upon a time she had regarded an evening alone with him as an entertainment superior to all others. He called her ridiculous names, talked to her in baby language; while a dozen times a day it became necessary for her to take down her back hair and do it up afresh. At the end of a month, as I have said, it was she who suggested a slight cessation of affection.'

'Had I been in her place,' said the Girton Girl, 'it would have been a separation I should have suggested. I should have hated him for the rest of my life.'

'For merely trying to agree with you?' I said.

'For showing me I was a fool for ever having wanted his affection,' replied the Girton Girl.

'You can generally,' said the Philosopher, 'make people ridiculous by taking them at their word.'

(Tea Table Talk.)

THE BILLIARD LESSON

There is a friend of mine, an old sea-captain. He is the sort of
man that when the three balls are lying in a straight line,
tucked up under the cushion, looks pleased; because then he
knows he can make a cannon and leave the red just where he
wants it. An Irish youngster named Malooney, a college chum
of Dick's, was staying with us; and the afternoon being wet,
the Captain said he would explain it to Malooney, how a young
man might practise billiards without any danger of cutting the
cloth. He taught him how to hold the cue, and he told him how
to make a bridge. Malooney was grateful, and worked for about
an hour. He did not show much promise. He is a powerfully
built young man, and he didn't seem able to get it into his head
that he wasn't playing cricket. Whenever he hit a little low the
result was generally lost ball. To save time – and damage to
furniture – Dick and I fielded for him. Dick stood at long-stop,
and I was short-slip. It was dangerous work, however, and
when Dick had caught him out twice running, we agreed that
we had won, and took him in to tea. In the evening – none of
the rest of us being keen to try our luck a second time – the
Captain said, that just for the joke of the thing he would give
Malooney eighty-five and play him a hundred up. To confess
the truth, I find no particular fun myself in playing billiards
with the Captain. The game consists, as far as I am concerned,
in walking round the table, throwing him back the balls, and
saying 'Good!' By the time my turn comes I don't seem to care
what happens: everything seems against me. He is a kind old
gentleman and he means well, but the tone in which he says
'Hard lines!' whenever I miss an easy stroke irritates me. I feel

I'd like to throw the balls at his head and fling the table out of window. I suppose it is that I am in a fretful state of mind, but the mere way in which he chalks his cue aggravates me. He carries his own chalk in his waistcoat pocket – as if our chalk wasn't good enough for him – and when he has finished chalking, he smooths the tip round with his finger and thumb and taps the cue against the table. 'Oh! go on with the game,' I want to say to him; 'don't be so full of tricks.'

The Captain led off with a miss in baulk. Malooney gripped his cue, drew in a deep breath, and let fly. The result was ten: a cannon and all three balls in the same pocket. As a matter of fact, he made the cannon twice; but the second time, as we explained to him, of course did not count.

'Good beginning!' said the Captain.

Malooney seemed pleased with himself, and took off his coat.

Malooney's ball missed the red on its first journey up the table by about a foot, but found it later on and sent it into a pocket.

'Ninety-nine plays nothing,' said Dick, who was marking. 'Better make it a hundred and fifty, hadn't we, Captain?'

'Well, I'd like to get in a shot.' said the Captain, 'before the game is over. Perhaps we had better make it a hundred and fifty, if Mr Malooney has no objection.'

'Whatever you think right, sir,' said Rory Malooney.

Malooney finished his break for twenty-two, leaving himself hanging over the middle pocket and the red tucked up in baulk.

'Nothing plays a hundred and eight,' said Dick.

'When I want the score,' said the Captain, 'I'll ask for it.'

'Beg pardon, sir,' said Dick.

'I hate a noisy game,' said the Captain.

The Captain, making up his mind without much waste of time, sent his ball under the cushion, six inches outside baulk.

'What will I do here?' asked Malooney.

'I don't know what you will do,' said the Captain; 'I'm waiting to see.'

Owing to the position of the ball, Malooney was unable to employ his whole strength. All he did that turn was to pocket the Captain's ball and leave himself under the bottom cushion, four inches from the red. The Captain said a nautical word, and gave another miss. Malooney squared up to the balls for a third time. They flew before him, panic-stricken. They banged against one another, came back and hit one another again for no reason whatever. The red, in particular, Malooney had succeeded apparently in frightening out of its wits. It is a stupid ball, generally speaking, our red – its one idea to get under a cushion and watch the game. With Malooney it soon found it was safe nowhere on the table. Its only hope was pockets. I may have been mistaken, my eye may have been deceived by the rapidity of the play, but it seemed to me that the red never waited to be hit. When it saw Malooney's ball coming for it at the rate of forty miles an hour, it just made for the nearest pocket. It rushed round the table looking for pockets. If, in its excitement, it passed an empty pocket, it turned back and crawled in. There were times when in its terror it jumped the table and took shelter under the sofa or behind the

It seemed to me that the red never waited to be hit.

sideboard. One began to feel sorry for the red.

The Captain had scored a legitimate thirty-eight, and Malooney had given him twenty-four, when it really seemed as if the Captain's chance had come. I could have scored myself as the balls were then.

'Sixty-two plays one hundred and twenty-eight. Now then, Captain, game in your hands,' said Dick.

We gathered round. The children left their play. It was a pretty picture: the bright young faces, eager with expectation, the old worn veteran squinting down his cue, as if afraid that watching Malooney's play might have given it the squirms.

'Now follow this,' I whispered to Malooney. 'Don't notice merely what he does, but try and understand why he does it. Any fool – after a little practice, that is – can hit a ball. But why do you hit it? What happens after you've hit it? What——'

'Hush,' said Dick.

The Captain drew his cue back and gently pushed it forward.

'Pretty stroke,' I whispered to Malooney; 'now, that's the sort——'

I offer, by way of explanation, that the Captain by this time was probably too full of bottled-up language to be master of his nerves. The ball travelled slowly past the red. Dick said afterwards that you couldn't have put so much as a sheet of paper between them.

It comforts a man, sometimes, when you tell him this; and at other times it only makes him madder.

It travelled on and passed the white – you could have put quite a lot of paper between it and the white – and dropped with a contented thud into the top left-hand pocket.

'Why does he do that?' Malooney whispered. Malooney has a singularly hearty whisper.

Dick and I got the women and children out of the room as quickly as we could, but of course Veronica managed to tumble over something on the way – Veronica would find something to tumble over in the desert of Sahara; and a few days later I overheard expressions, scorching their way through the nursery door, that made my hair rise up. I entered, and found Veronica standing on the table. Jumbo was sitting upon the music-stool. The poor dog himself was looking scared, though he must have heard a bit of language in his time, one way or another.

'Veronica,' I said, 'are you not ashamed of yourself? You wicked child, how dare you——'

'It's all right,' said Veronica. 'I don't really mean any harm. He's a sailor, and I have to talk to him like that, else he don't know he's being talked to.'

I pay hard-working, conscientious ladies to teach this child things right and proper for her to know. They tell her clever things that Julius Casear said; observations made by Marcus Aurelius that, pondered over, might help her to become a beautiful character. She complains that it produces a strange buzzy feeling in her head; and her mother argues that perhaps her brain is of the creative order, not intended to remember much – thinks that perhaps she is going to be something.

A good round-dozen oaths the Captain must have let fly before Dick and I succeeded in rolling her out of the room. She had only heard them once, yet, so far as I could judge, she had got them letter perfect.

The Captain, now no longer under the necessity of employing all his energies to suppress his natural instincts, gradually recovered form, and eventually the game stood at one hundred and forty-nine all, Malooney to play. The Captain had left the balls in a position that would have disheartened any other opponent than Malooney. To any other opponent than Malooney the Captain would have offered irritating sympathy. 'Afraid the balls are not rolling well for you to-night.' the Captain would have said; or, 'Sorry, sir, I don't seem to have left you very much.' To-night the Captain wasn't feeling playful.

'Well, if he scores off that!' said Dick.

'Short of locking up the balls and turning out the lights, I don't myself see how one is going to stop him,' sighed the Captain.

The Captain's ball was in hand. Malooney went for the red and hit – perhaps it would be more correct to say, frightened – it into a pocket. Malooney's ball, with the table to itself, then gave a solo performance, and ended up by breaking a window. It was what the lawyers call a nice point. What was the effect upon the score?

Malooney argued that, seeing he had pocketed the red before his own ball left the table, his three should be counted first, and that therefore he had won. Dick maintained that a ball that had ended up in a flower-bed couldn't be deemed to have scored anything. The Captain declined to assist. He said that, although he had been playing billiards for upwards of forty years, the incident was new to him. My own feeling was that of thankfulness that we had got through the game without anybody being really injured. We agreed that the person to decide the point would be the editor of *The Field*.

It remains still undecided. The Captain came into my study next morning. He said: 'If you haven't written that letter to *The Field*, don't mention my name. They know me on *The Field*. I would rather it did not get about that I have been playing with a man who cannot keep his ball within the four walls of a billiard-room.'

(They and I.)

ROBINA ON MARRIAGE

'I shall never marry,' said Robina. 'At least, I hope I shan't.'

'Why "hope"?' I asked.

'Because I hope I shall never be idiot enough,' she answered.
'I see it all so clearly. I wish I didn't. Love! it's only an ugly
thing with a pretty name. It will not be me that he will fall in
love with. He will not know me until it is too late. How can he?
It will be merely with the outside of me – my pink-and-white
skin, my rounded arms. I feel it sometimes when I see men
looking at me, and it makes me mad. And at other times the
admiration in their eyes pleases me. And that makes me
madder still.'

The moon had slipped behind the wood. She had risen, and,
leaning against the porch, was standing with her hands
clasped. I fancy she had forgotten me. She seemed to be
talking to the night.

'It's only a trick of Nature to make fools of us,' she said. 'He
will tell me I am all the world to him; that his love will outlive
the stars – will believe it himself at the time, poor fellow! He
will call me a hundred pretty names, will kiss my feet and
hands. And if I'm fool enough to listen to him, it may last' –
she laughed; it was rather an ugly laugh – 'six months; with
luck perhaps a year, if I'm careful not to go out in the east wind
and come home with a red nose, and never let him catch me in
curl papers. It will not be me that he will want: only my youth,
and the novelty of me, and the mystery. And when that is
gone——'

She turned to me. It was a strange face I saw then in the pale
light, quite a fierce little face. She laid her hands upon my

shoulders, and I felt them cold. 'What comes when it is dead?' she said. 'What follows? You must know. Tell me. I want the truth.'

Her vehemence had arisen so suddenly. The little girl I had set out to talk with was no longer there. To my bewilderment, it was a woman that was questioning me.

I drew her down beside me. But the childish face was still stern.

'I want the truth,' she said; so that I answered very gravely:

'When the passion is passed; when the glory and the wonder of Desire – Nature's eternal ritual of marriage, solemnizing, sanctifying it to her commands – is ended; when, sooner or later, some grey dawn finds you wandering bewildered in once familiar places, seeking vainly the lost palace of youth's dreams; when Love's frenzy is faded, like fragrance of the blossom, like the splendour of the dawn; there will remain to you, just what there was before – no more, no less. If passion was all you had to give to one another, God help you. You have had your hour of madness. It is finished. If greed of praise and worship was your price – well, you have had your payment. The bargain is complete. If mere hope to be made happy was your lure, one pities you. We do not make each other happy. Happiness is the gift of the gods, not of man. The secret lies within you, not without. What remains to you will depend not upon what you *thought,* but upon what you *are.* If behind the lover there was the man – behind the impossible goddess of his love-sick brain some honest, human woman, then life lies not behind you, but before you.

'Life is giving, not getting. That is the mistake we most of us set out with. It is the work that is the joy, not the wages; the game, not the score. The lover's delight is to yield, not to claim. The crown of motherhood is pain. To serve the State at cost of ease and leisure; to spend his thought and labour upon a hundred schemes, is the man's ambition. Life is doing, not having. It is to gain the peak the climber strives, not to possess it. Fools marry thinking what they are going to get out of it: good store of joys and pleasure, opportunities of self-indulgence, eternal soft caresses – the wages of the wanton. The rewards of marriage are toil, duty, responsibility – manhood, womanhood. Love's baby talk you will have outgrown. You will no longer be his "Goddess", "Angel", "Popsy Wopsy", "Queen of his heart". There are finer names than these: wife, mother, priestess in the temple of humanity. Marriage is renunciation, the sacrifice of self upon the altar of the race. "A trick of Nature" you call it. Perhaps. But a trick of Nature compelling you to surrender yourself to the purposes of God.'

I fancy we must have sat in silence for quite a long while; for the moon, creeping upward past the wood, had flooded the fields again with light before Robina spoke.

'Then all love is needless,' she said, 'we could do better without it, choose with more discretion. If it is only something that worries us for a little while and then passes, what is the sense of it?'

'You could ask the same question of Life itself,' I said; '"something that worries us for a little while, then passes." Perhaps the "worry," as you call it, has its uses. Volcanic upheavals are necessary to the making of a world. Without them the ground would remain rock-bound, unfitted for its purposes. Love serves to the making of man and woman. It does not die, it takes new shape. The blossom fades as the fruit forms. The passion passes to give place to peace. The trembling lover has become the helper, the comforter, the husband.'

'But the failures,' Robina persisted; 'I do not mean the silly or the wicked people; but the people who begin by really loving one another, only to end in disliking – almost hating one another. How do *they* get there?'

'Sit down,' I said, 'and I will tell you a story.'

(They and I.)

DREAM CHILDREN

'Why didn't you have better children?' sobbed Robina; 'we are none of us any good to you.'

'You are not the children I wanted, I confess,' I answered.

'That's a nice kind thing to say!' retorted Robina indignantly.

'I wanted such charming children,' I explained – 'my idea of charming children; the children I had imagined for myself. Even as babies you disappointed me.'

Robina looked astonished.

'You, Robina, were the most disappointing,' I complained. 'Dick was a boy. One does not calculate upon boy angels; and by the time Veronica arrived I had got more used to things. But I was so excited when you came. The Little Mother and I would steal at night into the nursery. "Isn't it wonderful," the Little Mother would whisper, "to think it all lies hidden there: the little tiresome child, the sweetheart they will one day take away from us, the wife, the mother?" "I am glad it is a girl," I would whisper; "I shall be able to watch her grow into womanhood. Most of the girls one comes across in books strike one as not perhaps quite true to life. It will give me such an advantage to have a girl of my own. I shall keep a note-book, with a lock and key, devoted to her."'

'Did you?' asked Robina.

'I put it away,' I answered; 'there were but a few pages written on. It came to me quite early in your life that you were not going to be the model heroine. I was looking for the picture baby, the clean, thoughtful baby, with its magical, mystical smile. I wrote poetry about you, Robina, but you would slobber and howl. Your little nose was always having to be wiped, and somehow the poetry did not seem to fit you. You were at your best when you were asleep, but you would not even sleep when it was expected of you. I think, Robina, that the fellows who draw the pictures for the comic journals of the man in his night-shirt with the squalling baby in his arms must all be single men. The married man sees only sadness in the design. It is not the mere discomfort. If the little creature were ill or in pain we should not think of that. It is the reflection that we, who meant so well, have brought into the world just an ordinary fretful human creature with a nasty temper of its own: that is the tragedy, Robina. And then you grew into a little girl. I wanted the soulful little girl with the fathomless eyes, who would steal to me at twilight and question me concerning life's conundrums.'

'But I used to ask you questions,' grumbled Robina, 'and you would tell me not to be silly.'

'Don't you understand, Robina?' I answered. 'I am not blaming you, I am blaming myself. We are like children who plant seeds in a garden, and then are angry with the flowers because they are not what we expected. You were a dear little girl; I see that now, looking back. But not the little girl I had in my mind. So I missed you, thinking of the little girl you were not. We do that all our lives, Robina. We are always looking for the flowers that do not grow, passing by, trampling underfoot, the blossoms round about us. It was the same with Dick. I wanted a naughty boy. Well, Dick was naughty, no one can say that he was not. But it was not my naughtiness. I was prepared for his robbing orchards. I rather hoped he would rob orchards. All the high-spirited boys in books rob orchards, and become great men. But there were not any orchards handy. We happened to be living in Chelsea at the time he ought to have been robbing orchards: that, of course, was my fault. I did not think of that. He stole a bicycle that a lady had left outside the tea-room in Battersea Park, he and another boy, the son of a

common barber, who shaved people for three-halfpence. I am a Republican in theory, but it grieved me that a son of mine could be drawn to such companionship. They contrived to keep it for a week – till the police found it one night, artfully hidden behind bushes. Logically, I do not see why stealing apples should be noble and stealing bicycles should be mean, but it struck me that way at the time. It was not the particular steal I had been hoping for.

'I wanted him wild; the hero of the book was ever in his college days a wild young man. Well, he was wild. It cost me three hundred pounds to keep that breach of promise case out of Court; I had never imagined a breach of promise case. Then he got drunk, and bonneted a bishop in mistake for a "bull-dog". I didn't mind the bishop. That by itself would have been wholesome fun. But to think that a son of mine should have been drunk!'

'He has never been drunk since,' pleaded Robina. 'He had only three glasses of champagne and a liqueur: it was the liqueur – he was not used to it. He got into the wrong set. You cannot in college belong to the wild set without getting drunk occasionally.'

'Perhaps not,' I admitted. 'In the book the wild young man drinks without ever getting drunk. Maybe there is a difference between life and the book. In the book you enjoy your fun, but contrive somehow to escape the licking: in life the licking is the only thing sure. It was the wild young man of fiction I was looking for, who, a fortnight before the exam, ties a wet towel round his head, drinks strong tea, and passes easily with honours. He tried the wet towel, he tells me. It never would keep in its place. Added to which it gave him neuralgia; while the strong tea gave him indigestion. I used to picture myself the proud, indulgent father lecturing him for his wildness – turning away at some point in the middle of my tirade to hide a smile. There was never any smile to hide. I feel that he has behaved disgracefully, wasting his time and my money.'

'He is going to turn over a new leaf,' said Robina: 'I am sure he will make an excellent farmer.'

'I did not want a farmer,' I explained; 'I wanted a Prime Minister. Children, Robina, are very disappointing. Veronica is all wrong. I like a mischievous child. I like reading stories of mischievous children: they amuse me. But not the child who puts a pound of gunpowder into a red-hot fire, and escapes with her life by a miracle.'

'And yet, I daresay,' suggested Robina, 'that if one put it into a book – I mean that if you put it into a book, it would read amusingly.'

'Likely enough,' I agreed. 'Other people's troubles can always be amusing. As it is, I shall be in a state of anxiety for the next six months, wondering, every moment that she is out of my sight, what new devilment she is up to. The Little Mother will be worried out of her life, unless we can keep it from her.'

'Children will be children,' murmured Robina, meaning to be comforting.

'That is what I am complaining of, Robina. We are always hoping that ours won't be. She is full of faults, Veronica, and they are not always nice faults. She is lazy – lazy is not the word for it.'

'She is lazy,' Robina was compelled to admit.

'There are other faults she might have had and welcome,' I pointed out; 'faults I could have taken an interest in and liked her all the better for. You children are so obstinate. You will choose your own faults. Veronica is not truthful always. I wanted a family of little George Washingtons, who could not tell a lie. Veronica can. To get herself out of trouble – and provided there is any hope of anybody believing her – she does.'

'We all of us used to when we were young,' Robina maintained; 'Dick used to, I used to. It is a common fault with children.'

'I know it is,' I answered. 'I did not want a child with common faults. I wanted something all my own. I wanted you, Robina, to be my ideal daughter. I had a girl in my mind that I am sure would have been charming. You are not a bit like her. I don't say she was perfect, she had her failings, but they were such delightful failings – much better than yours, Robina. She had a temper – a woman without a temper is insipid; but it was that kind of temper that made you love her all the more. Yours doesn't, Robina. I wish you had not been in such a hurry, and had left me to arrange your temper for you. We should all of us have preferred mine. It had all the attractions of a temper without the drawbacks of the ordinary temper.'

'Couldn't use it up, I suppose, for yourself, Pa?' suggested Robina.

'It was a lady's temper,' I explained. 'Besides,' as I asked her, 'what is wrong with the one I have?'

'Nothing,' answered Robina. Yet her tone conveyed doubt.

(They and I.)

THE WINDOW AJAR

Mr Airlie, picking daintily at his food, continued his stories: of philanthropists who paid starvation wages: of feminists who were a holy terror to their women folk: of socialists who travelled first-class and spent their winters in Egypt or Monaco: of stern critics of public morals who preferred the society of youthful affinities to the continued company of elderly wives: of poets who wrote divinely about babies' feet and whose children hated them.

'Do you think it's all true?' Joan whispered to her host.

He shrugged his shoulders. 'No reason why it shouldn't be,' he said. 'I've generally found him right.'

'I've never been able myself,' he continued, 'to understand the Lord's enthusiasm for David. I suppose it was the Psalms that did it.'

Joan was about to offer comment, but was struck dumb with astonishment on hearing McKean's voice: it seemed he could talk. He was telling of an old Scotch peasant farmer. A mean, cantankerous old cuss whose curious pride it was that he had never given anything away. Not a crust, nor a sixpence, nor a rag; and never would. Many had been the attempts to make him break his boast: some for the joke of the thing and some for the need; but none had ever succeeded. It was his one claim to distinction and he guarded it.

One evening it struck him that the milk-pail, standing just inside the window, had been tampered with. Next day he marked with a scratch the inside of the pan, and returning later, found the level of the milk had sunk by half an inch. So he hid himself and waited; and at twilight the next day the window was stealthily pushed open and two small terror-haunted eyes peered round the room. They satisfied themselves that no one was about and a tiny hand clutching a cracked jug was thrust swiftly in and dipped into the pan; and the window softly closed.

He knew the thief, the grandchild of an old bedridden dame who lived some miles away on the edge of the moor. The old man stood long, watching the small cloaked figure till it was lost in the darkness. It was not till he lay upon his dying bed that he confessed it. But each evening, from that day, he would steal into the room and see to it himself that the window was left ajar.

(All Roads Lead to Calvary.)

One evening it struck him that the milk-pail, standing just inside the window, had been tampered with.

THE MAKERS OF WAR

One topic that never lost its interest was: Who made wars? Who hounded the people into them, and kept them there, tearing at one another's throats? They never settled it.

'God knows I didn't want it, speaking personally,' said a German prisoner one day, with a laugh. 'I had been working at a printing business sixteen hours a day for seven years. It was just beginning to pay me, and now my wife writes me that she has had to shut the place up and sell the machinery to keep them all from starving.'

'But couldn't you have done anything to stop it?' demanded a Frenchman, lying next to him. 'All your millions of Socialists, what were they up to? What went wrong with the Internationale, the Universal Brotherhood of Labour, and all that Tra-la-la?'

The German laughed again. 'Oh, they know their business,' he answered. 'You have your glass of beer and go to bed, and when you wake up in the morning you find war has been declared; and you keep your mouth shut – unless you want to be shot for a traitor. Not that it would have made much difference,' he added. 'I admit that. The ground had been too well prepared. England was envious of our trade. King Edward had been plotting our destruction. Our papers were full of translations from yours, talking about "*La Revanche!*" We were told that you had been lending money to Russia to enable her to build railways, and that when they were complete France and Russia would fall upon us suddenly. "The Fatherland in danger!" It may be lies or it may not; what is one to do? What would you have done – even if you could have done anything?'

'He's right,' said a dreamy-eyed looking man, laying down
the book he had been reading. 'We should have done just the
same. "My country, right or wrong." After all, it is an ideal.'

A dark, black-bearded man raised himself painfully upon his
elbow. He was a tailor in the Rue Parnesse, and prided himself
on a decided resemblance to Victor Hugo.

'It's a noble ideal,' he said. '*La Patrie!* The great Mother.
Right or wrong, who shall dare to harm her? Yes, if it was she
who rose up in her majesty and called to us.' He laughed.
'What does it mean in reality: Germania, Italia, La France,
Britannia? Half a score of pompous old muddlers with their fat
wives egging them on: sons of the fools before them; talkers
who have wormed themselves into power by making frothy
speeches and fine promises. My Country!' he laughed again.
'Look at them. Can't you see their swelling paunches and their
flabby faces? Half a score of ambitious politicians, gouty old
financiers, bald-headed old toffs, with their waxed moustaches
and false teeth. That's what we mean when we talk about "My
Country": a pack of selfish, soulless, muddle-headed old men.
And whether they're right or whether they're wrong, our duty
is to fight at their bidding – to bleed for them, to die for them,
that they may grow more sleek and prosperous.' He sank back
on his pillow with another laugh.

Sometimes they agreed it was the newspapers that made war
– that fanned every trivial difference into a vital question of
national honour – that, whenever there was any fear of peace,
re-stoked the fires of hatred with their never-failing stories of
atrocities. At other times they decided it was the capitalists, the
traders, scenting profit for themselves. Some held it was the
politicians, dreaming of going down to history as Richelieus or
as Bismarcks. A popular theory was that cause for war was
always discovered by the ruling classes whenever there seemed
danger that the workers were getting out of hand. In war, you
put the common people back in their place, revived in them the
habits of submission and obedience. Napoleon the Little, it

was argued, had started the war of 1870 with that idea. Russia had welcomed the present war as an answer to the Revolution that was threatening Czardom. Others contended it was the great munition industries, aided by the military party; the officers impatient for opportunities of advancement, the strategists eager to put their theories to the test. A few of the more philosophical shrugged their shoulders. It was the thing itself that sooner or later was bound to go off of its own accord. Half every country's energy, half every country's time and money was spent in piling up explosives. In every country envy and hatred of every other country was preached as a religion. They called it patriotism. Sooner or later the spark fell.

A wizened little man had been listening to it all one day. He had a curiously rat-like face, with round, red, twinkling eyes, and a long, pointed nose that twitched as he talked.

'I'll tell you who makes all the wars,' he said. 'It's you and me, my dears: we make the wars. We love them. That's why we open our mouths and swallow all the twaddle that the papers give us; and cheer the fine, black-coated gentlemen when they tell us it's our sacred duty to kill Germans, or Italians, or Russians, or anybody else. We are just crazy to kill something: it doesn't matter what. If it's to be Germans, we

shout 'A Berlin!'; and if it's to be Russians we cheer for Liberty. I was in Paris at the time of the Fashoda trouble. How we hissed the English in the cafés. And how they glared back at us! They were just as eager to kill us. Who makes a dog fight? Why, the dog. Anybody can do it. Who could make us fight each other, if we didn't want to? Not all the King's horses and all the King's men. No, my dears, it's we make the wars. You and me, my dears.'

(All Roads Lead to Calvary.)

ALL ROADS LEAD TO CALVARY

'All roads lead to Calvary.' It was curious how the words had dwelt with her, till gradually they had become a part of her creed. She remembered how at first they had seemed to her a threat, chilling her with fear. They had grown to be a promise: a hope held out to all. The road to Calvary! It was the road to life. By the giving up of self we gained God.

And suddenly a great peace came to her. One was not alone in the fight. God was with us: the great Comrade. The evil and the cruelty all round her: she was no longer afraid of it. God was coming. Beyond the menace of the passing day, black with the war's foul aftermath of evil dreams and hatreds, she saw the breaking of the distant dawn. The devil should not always triumph. God was gathering His labourers.

God was conquering. Unceasing through the ages, God's voice had crept round man, seeking entry. Through the long darkness of that dim beginning, when man knew no law but self, unceasing, God had striven: until at last one here and there, emerging from the brute, had heard – had listened to the voice of love and pity, and in that hour, unknowing, had built to God a temple in the wilderness.

Labourers together with God. The mighty host of those who through the ages had heard the voice of God and had made answer. The men and women in all lands who had made room in their hearts for God. Still nameless, scattered, unknown to one another: still powerless as yet against the world's foul law of hate, they should continue to increase and multiply, until one day they should speak with God's voice and should be heard. And a new world should be created.

192

God. The tireless Spirit of eternal creation, the Spirit of
Love. What else was it that out of formlessness had shaped the
spheres, had planned the orbits of the suns. The law of gravity
we named it. What was it but another name for Love, the
yearning of like for like, the calling to one another of the stars.
What else but Love had made the worlds, had gathered
together the waters, had fashioned the dry land. The cohesion
of elements, so we explained it. The clinging of like to like.
The brotherhood of the atoms.

God. The Eternal Creator. Out of matter, lifeless void, He
had moulded His worlds, had ordered His endless firmament.
It was finished. The greater task remained: the Universe of
mind, of soul. Out of man it should be created. God in man
and man in God: made in like image: fellow labourers together
with one another: together they should build it. Out of the
senseless strife and discord, above the chaos and the tumult
should be heard the new command: 'Let there be Love.'

(All Roads Lead to Calvary.)

THE MUSIC HALL OF THE OLD REGIME

It was not until I was nearly seventeen that the idea occurred to me to visit a Music Hall again. Then, having regard to my double capacity of 'Man about Town' and journalist (for I had written a letter to *The Era,* complaining of the way pit doors were made to open, and it had been inserted), I felt I had no longer any right to neglect acquaintanceship with so important a feature in the life of the people. Accordingly, one Saturday night, I wended my way to the 'Pav.'; and there the first person that I ran against was my uncle. He laid a heavy hand upon my shoulder, and asked me, in severe tones, what I was doing there. I felt this to be an awkward question, for it would have been useless trying to make him understand my real motives (one's own relations are never sympathetic), and I was somewhat nonplussed for an answer, until the reflection occurred to me: What was *he* doing there? This riddle I, in my turn, propounded to him, with the result that we entered into a treaty, by the terms of which it was agreed that no future reference should be made to the meeting by either of us – especially not in the presence of my aunt – and the compact was ratified according to the usual custom, my uncle paying the necessary expenses.

In those days we sat, some four or six of us, round a little table, on which were placed our drinks. Now we have to balance them upon a narrow ledge; and ladies, as they pass, dip the ends of their cloaks into them, and gentlemen stir them up for us with the ferrules of their umbrellas, or else sweep them off into our laps with their coat tails, saying as they do so, 'Oh, I beg your pardon.'

Also, in those days, there were 'chairmen' – affable gentlemen, who would drink anything at anybody's expense, and drink any quantity of it, and never seem to get any fuller. I was introduced to a Music Hall chairman once, and when I said to him, 'What is your drink?' he took up the 'List of beverages' that lay before him, and, opening it, waved his hand lightly across its entire contents, from clarets, past champagnes and spirits, down to liqueurs. 'That's my drink, my boy,' said he. There was nothing narrow-minded or exclusive about his tastes.

It was the chairman's duty to introduce the artists. 'Ladies and gentlemen,' he would shout, in a voice that united the musical characteristics of a fog-horn and a steam saw, 'Miss 'Enerietta Montressor, the popular serio-comic will now happear.' These announcements were invariably received with great applause by the chairman himself, and generally with chilling indifference by the rest of the audience.

It was also the privilege of the chairman to maintain order, and reprimand evil-doers. This he usually did very effectively, employing for the purpose language both fit and forcible. One chairman that I remember seemed, however, to be curiously deficient in the necessary qualities for this part of his duty. He was a mild and sleepy little man, and, unfortunately, he had to preside over an exceptionally rowdy audience at a small hall in the South-East district. On the night that I was present there occurred a great disturbance. 'Joss Jessop, the Monarch of Mirth,' a gentleman evidently high in local request, was, for some reason or other, not forthcoming, and in his place the management proposed to offer a female performer on the zithern, one Signorina Ballatino.

The little chairman made the announcement in a nervous, deprecatory tone, as if he were rather ashamed of it himself. 'Ladies and gentlemen,' he began, – the poor are staunch sticklers for etiquette: I overheard a small child explaining to her mother one night in Three Colts Street, Limehouse, that she could not get into the house because there was a 'lady' on the doorstep, drunk, – 'Signorina Ballatino, the world-renowned——'

Here a voice from the gallery requested to know what had become of 'Old Joss,' and was greeted by loud cries of ''Ear, 'ear.'

The chairman, ignoring the interruption, continued:

'——the world-renowned performer on the zither——'

'On the whoter?' came in tones of plaintive inquiry from the back of the hall.

'*Hon* the zither,' retorted the chairman, waxing mildly ir.dignant; he meant zithern, but he called it a zither. 'A hinstrument well known to anybody as 'as 'ad any learning.'

This sally was received with much favour, and a gentleman who claimed to be acquainted with the family history of the interrupter begged the chairman to excuse that ill-bred person on the ground that his mother used to get drunk with the twopence a week and never sent him to school.

Cheered by this breath of popularity, our little president endeavoured to complete his introduction of the Signorina. He again repeated that she was the world-renowned performer on the zithern; and, undeterred by the audible remark of a lady in the pit to the effect that she'd 'never 'eard on 'er,' added:

'She will now, ladies and gentlemen, with your kind permission, give you examples of the——'

'Blow yer zither!' here cried out the gentleman who had started the agitation; 'we want Joss Jessop.'

This was the signal for much cheering and shrill whistling, in the midst of which a wag with a piping voice suggested as a reason for the favourite's non-appearance that he had not been paid his last week's salary.

A temporary lull occurred at this point; and the chairman, seizing the opportunity to complete his oft-impeded speech, suddenly remarked, 'songs of the Sunny South'; and immediately sat down and began hammering upon the table.

Then Signorina Ballatino, clothed in the costume of the

Sunny South, where clothes are less essential than in these colder climes, skipped airily forward, and was most ungallantly greeted with a storm of groans and hisses. Her beloved instrument was unfeelingly alluded to as a pie-dish, and she was advised to take it back and get the penny on it. The chairman, addressed by his Christian name of 'Jimmee', was told to lie down and let her sing him to sleep. Every time she attempted to start playing shouts were raised for Joss.

At length the chairman, overcoming his evident disinclination to take any sort of hand whatever in the game, rose and gently hinted at the desirability of silence. The suggestion not meeting with any support, he proceeded to adopt sterner measures. He addressed himself personally to the ringleader of the rioters, the man who had first championed the cause of the absent Joss. This person was a brawny individual, who, judging from appearances, followed in his business hours the calling of a coalheaver. 'Yes, sir,' said the chairman, pointing a finger towards him, where he sat in the front row of the gallery; 'you, sir, in the flannel shirt. I can see you. Will you allow this lady to give her entertainment?'

'No,' answered he of the coalheaving profession, in stentorian tones.

'Then, sir,' said the little chairman, working himself up into a state suggestive of Jove about to launch a thunderbolt – 'then, sir, all I can say is that you are no gentleman.'

This was a little too much, or rather a good deal too little, for the Signorina Ballatino. She had hitherto been standing in a meek attitude of pathetic appeal, wearing a fixed smile of ineffable sweetness; but she evidently felt that she could go a bit farther than that herself, even if she was a lady. Calling the chairman 'an old messer', and telling him for Gawd's sake to shut up if that was all he could do for his living, she came down to the front, and took the case into her own hands.

She did not waste time on the rest of the audience. She went direct for that coal-heaver, and thereupon ensued a slanging match the memory of which sends a thrill of admiration through me even to this day. It was a battle worthy of the gods. He was a heaver of coals, quick and ready beyond his kind. During many years sojourn East and South, in the course of many wanderings from Billingsgate to Limehouse Hole, from Petticoat Lane to Whitechapel Road; out of eel-pie shop and penny gaff; out of tavern and street and court and doss-house, he had gathered together slang words and terms and phrases, and they came back to him now, and he stood up against her manfully.

But as well might the lamb stand up against the eagle, when the shadow of its wings falls across the green pastures, and the

Took the case into her own hands.

wind flies before its dark oncoming. At the end of two minutes he lay gasping, dazed, and speechless.

Then she began.

She announced her intention of 'wiping down the bloomin' 'all' with him, and making it respectable; and, metaphorically speaking, that is what she did. Her tongue hit him between the eyes, and knocked him down and trampled on him. It curled round and round him like a whip, and then it uncurled and wound the other way. It seized him by the scruff of his neck, and tossed him up into the air, and caught him as he descended, and flung him to the ground, and rolled him on it. It played round him like forked lightning, and blinded him. It danced and shrieked about him like a host of whirling fiends, and he tried to remember a prayer, and could not. It touched him lightly on the sole of his foot and the crown of his head, and his hair stood up straight, and his limbs grew stiff. The people sitting near him drew away, not feeling it safe to be near, and left him alone, surrounded by space, and language.

It was the most artistic piece of work of its kind that I have ever heard. Every phrase she flung at him seemed to have been woven on purpose to entangle him and to embrace in its choking folds his people and his gods, to strangle with its threads his every hope, ambition, and belief. Each term she put upon him clung to him like a garment, and fitted him without a crease. The last name that she called him one felt to be, until one heard the next, the one name that he ought to have been christened by.

For five and three-quarter minutes by the clock she spoke, and never for one instant did she pause or falter; and in the whole of that onslaught there was only one weak spot.

That was when she offered to make a better man than he was out of a Guy Fawkes and a lump of coal. You felt that one lump of coal would not have been sufficient.

At the end, she gathered herself together for one supreme effort, and hurled at him an insult so bitter with scorn, so sharp with insight into his career and character, so heavy with prophetic curse, that strong men drew and held their breath while it passed over them, and women hid their faces and shivered.

Then she folded her arms, and stood silent; and the house, from floor to ceiling, rose and cheered her until there was no more breath left in its lungs.

In that one night she stepped from oblivion into success. She is now a famous 'artiste'.

But she does not call herself Signorina Ballatino, and she does not play upon the zither. Her name has a homelier sound, and her speciality is the delineation of coster character.

(John Ingerfield.)